Lessons
from Longford

Important Disclaimer

4491

Lessons from Longford

The Esso Gas Plant Explosion

Andrew Hopkins

CCH AUSTRALIA LIMITED

GPO Box 4072, Sydney, NSW 2001
Head Office North Ryde
Ph: (02) 9857 1300 Fax: (02) 9857 1600
Customer Support Ph: 1 300 300 224 Fax: 1 300 306 224

About CCH Australia Limited

CCH Australia Limited is part of a leading global organisation publishing in many countries.

CCH began business in Australia in 1969 and quickly established a solid reputation as the country's leading tax publisher. Today our scope is much broader, and our product range is constantly being expanded to meet customer needs.

CCH publications cover a wide variety of topical areas, including tax, company law, accounting, contract law, conveyancing, human resources, industrial law, occupational health and safety, torts and training. CCH is committed to identifying and integrating new technologies into its products.

Our clients include barristers, solicitors, accountants, human resources managers, OHS specialists, business people and students. We aim to provide up-to-date, accurate, authoritative, knowledge-based, practical information which customers can easily and quickly apply to their own specific circumstances.

Enquiries are welcome on 1300 300 224.

National Library of Australia Cataloguing in Publication Data

Hopkins, Andrew, 1945-.

Lessons from Longford: the Esso gas plant explosion.

     Bibliography.
     Includes index.
     ISBN 1 86468 422 4

     1. Esso Australia. Longford Plant. - Explosion, 1998.
     2. Gas industry - Accidents - Victoria - La Trobe River Valley.
     3. Gas industry - Victoria - La Trobe River Valley -
     Safety measures. 4. Industry safety - Victoria.
     I. Title.

363.11966574099456

Cover design and execution by Never a Dull Moment, St Leonards, New South Wales.

Typeset by Reolon Pty Ltd, 5 Arrunga Road, Arcadia, New South Wales.

©2000 **CCH** Australia Limited

First Published .... April 2000   Reprinted .... March 2001, January 2002

Wholly set up and printed in Australia

Preface

How does a sociologist come to write a book about a gas plant accident? How was it that I was called as an expert witness at an inquiry where engineering expertise was required to understand exactly what happened? These are questions I am often asked and it is perhaps worth recording some answers here.

It goes back to a book of mine which was published just as the Longford Royal Commission began in December 1998. That book was about another major accident, an explosion in a coal mine in central Queensland, and it focused on the cultural and organisational aspects of the accident, matters which are of central concern to sociology.

I sent a copy to a union health and safety officer in Melbourne, Yossi Berger, who recognised immediately its relevance to Longford. He passed it on to Mark Dean, the barrister who had been briefed to represent the Victorian Trades Hall Council at the inquiry. Mark asked me for advice in preparing the Trades Hall Council submission and asked that I write a statement on the sociological aspects of the accident and on the need for regulatory reform.

Parties such as the Trades Hall Council have no automatic right to call witnesses or submit witness statements; counsel assisting the Commission is the person who organises and presents the evidence. Mark and co-counsel Rachel Doyle were able to persuade him of the relevance of my evidence and the result was that counsel assisting formally tendered my statement. This meant, of course, that other parties had also to take note. Esso, in particular, objected to some of my observations and had me called so that I might be cross-examined. The cross-examination did not, however, discredit my evidence.

The end result was that findings about the cultural and organisational causes of accidents were brought formally to the attention of the Commission. It is most unusual in this country for a sociologist to be called as an expert witness in a disaster or coronial inquiry, but in accepting my evidence the Commission was acknowledging the value of the sociological approach to its inquiry. The present book is a much extended and elaborated version of the statement I made to the Commission. Readers will thus be in a position to make their own judgements about the value of sociology for understanding accidents.

Andrew Hopkins
Canberra
(Andrew.Hopkins@anu.edu.au)
April 2000

v

Contents

Chapter

1

Introduction

Things happened on that day that no one had seen at Longford before. A steel cylinder sprang a leak that let liquid hydrocarbon spill onto the ground. A dribble at first, but then, over the course of the morning it developed into a cascade ... Ice formed on pipework that normally was too hot to touch. Pumps that never stopped, ceased flowing and refused to start. Storage tank liquid levels that were normally stable plummeted ... I was in Control Room One when the first explosion ripped apart a 14-tonne steel vessel, 25 metres from where I was standing. It sent shards of steel, dust, debris and liquid hydrocabon into the atmosphere (The Age, 30/9/99).

These are the words of the operator whom Esso blamed for the accident at its gas plant at Longford, Victoria on 25 September 1998, an accident which killed two men, injured eight others and cut Melbourne's gas supply for two weeks.

The Royal Commission took the view that neither this man nor any of the others present on that day was at fault, for none of them understood the significance of the mysterious events they were witnessing. The fault was Esso's. The company had "failed to take measures which were plainly practicable", measures which it "could and should" have taken.

This book is an attempt to understand what went wrong at Longford and why it was that the Royal Commission came so firmly to the view that Esso was to blame and that the accident was practicably preventable. There are, as we shall see, lessons for both companies and governments in this story.

As I studied the causes of the explosion at Longford I was increasingly struck by parallels with a disaster I had previously studied (Hopkins, 1999). Four years earlier, Moura coal mine in central Queensland exploded with the loss of 11 lives. In both cases there were warning signs which management ignored, communication failures, systematic lack of attention to major hazards, auditing failures and a failure to learn from previous experience. Despite the very different technologies of gas plants and coal mines, it was apparent that fundamentally similar organisational deficiencies were involved in both events.

But there were also some striking differences. Whereas the Royal Commission pulled no punches in attributing fault to Esso, the Moura inquiry failed even to comment on the role of the operating company, BHP, let alone find fault with it. This is an intriguing difference and exploring it will bring out the significance of the Longford accident.

Although Longford is over 200 kilometres from Melbourne, the accident directly affected the great majority of Melbourne residents. Many thousands of people whose workplaces relied on gas were laid off, at financial cost to themselves and their employers. Moreover, Melbournians were subjected to a variety of inconveniences, among them the physical discomfort of cold showers. This collective experience of adversity generated a spirit of almost wartime solidarity. The majority of Victorians thus had a personal interest in the crisis and a continuing interest, even after its resolution, in finding someone to blame. This was a politically dangerous situation for the government of the day. Gas is a basic utility, an essential service, and the failure of supply could easily be seen as the responsibility of government. The matter was especially sensitive given that the government had recently taken the controversial step of privatising the State's gas distribution network. It was imperative, from the government's point of view, that any suggestion that it was responsible be headed off, if possible by blaming Esso. A coronial investigation had already begun and a prosecution by WorkCover could be expected to follow in due course. But the ordinary processes of law were far too slow and uncertain to be relied upon, and so the government took the extraordinary step of appointing a Royal Commission to investigate and report within three months on the causes of the accident. The Commission was asked, in particular, to investigate whether legal violations by Esso had contributed to the accident. Accordingly, it did not confine itself to taking evidence from staff at Longford, but interrogated several of the directors and senior managers from Esso's head office in Melbourne. The Commission was not specifically asked to investigate the role of Esso's parent company, Exxon, presumably because no political purpose would be served. I shall argue later that Exxon's practices indeed contributed to the accident.

An industrial accident in which two workers had been killed would not normally stimulate such a vigorous response by government. But this was no ordinary industrial accident. It had political and economic consequences which went way beyond the workplace.

Compare this with Moura. The accident occurred in a remote part of Queensland and had no direct effect on any major population centre. The death of eleven miners was certainly a shock to the collective consciousness, but because most Queenslanders had no personal involvement and no direct interest in finding a party to blame, the political fallout could be expected to be minimal. In these circumstances the ordinary processes of law could be allowed to operate. The Queensland *Coal Mining Act* specifies that an inquiry be held into "the nature and cause" of every mining accident causing death or serious bodily injury, and the Moura inquiry was conducted on this basis. The Act does not require that the role of the operating company be considered, and so it wasn't. The highest ranking company official who appeared as a witness was the mine manager; no one from BHP Coal's head office in Brisbane gave evidence. Moreover, the Act does not ask inquiries to find fault, and so the Moura inquiry didn't. In fact, it scrupulously avoided questions of blame, working on the theory that any attempt to identify fault would make witnesses unwilling to cooperate and thus the task of accident investigation more difficult. The chair of the inquiry told lawyers for the parties at one point:

> *What I will not do is stand by and see any witness crucified because he has come forward and is prepared to take any criticism of his shortcomings. Whatever your attitude to the veracity of any witness ... you are not going to shoot the*

messenger. That is not the purpose of this inquiry. The purpose is to determine the nature and cause and formulate recommendations to prevent a recurrence.

This raises the issue of whether the Longford Commission was hampered in getting at the facts by its fault-finding function. There is no doubt that Esso did its level best to avoid being incriminated. This is presumably why it chose to place its own accident investigation in the hands of outside lawyers and then to claim legal professional privilege, that is, that anything to do with that investigation, particularly any finding, was confidential because of the lawyer-client relationship. According to critics, this is standard Exxon practice around the world, whenever Exxon or its affiliates suffer major accidents, and it has prevented at least one coronial investigation in the past from getting to the truth (Michael Ford, *7.30 Report*, 3/5/99).

The Victorian Government had foreseen this strategy. It was not going to let Esso off the hook so easily and changed the *Evidence Act* just prior to the hearing to enable the Commission to over-ride the claim of privilege (see section 19D). But as soon as the occasion arose at the Commission, Esso indicated it wished to challenge the legislation in the Federal Court. Months later the Federal Court found against Esso, but the company thereupon appealed to the High Court. As a result of these delays the Commission had not been able to discover anything about Esso's own accident investigation by the time it concluded its hearings. But by this time the Commission had uncovered the causes of the explosion to its own satisfaction. Esso's victory was therefore a hollow one.

The success of the Royal Commission in getting at the facts was due in part to the enormous investigative resources available to it. Where inquiries are not as well resourced the strategy of using lawyer-client privilege may indeed result in the effective suppression of evidence. This is not, however, an argument for setting up inquiries which explicitly avoid questions of corporate fault. Companies will always have an eye to the possibility of later litigation and must be expected to behave at any inquiry as if they are on trial. Esso would have set up its lawyer-client relationship regardless of the Commission's terms of reference (see further, Baram, 1997).

The themes of this book

A number of themes or issues are woven through this book and it is worth flagging them now so that the reader will recognise them when they appear.

Practicable preventability

Consider the sense of bafflement conveyed in the operator's words with which this chapter began. For this man and for all those on site that day, the accident was unexpected, unpredictable and a result of technological complexity beyond their comprehension. And yet the Commission found it to have been practicably preventable. Are accidents in technologically complex environments ultimately inevitable or are they realistically preventable?

The question is raised in a particularly dramatic way by an incident in which a UK airliner suddenly lost oil pressure in both engines and was forced to make an emergency landing. The problem was traced to flawed maintenance practices. According to one respected accident analyst, the incident had "found its way through small chinks in the system's extensive armour" (Reason, 1997:22). The imagery suggests inevitability. On the other hand, when the matter came to court the airline was convicted for "an act of crass negligence" (*The Times*, 26/7/96). The court's conclusion was that the incident was reasonably foreseeable and practicably preventable. It is clear that the same event can be seen in very different ways.

This is not the place for a general discussion of this conundrum. Suffice it to say that the question of technological inevitability versus practicable preventability lies at the heart of this book.

Cause

Accident analyses abound with references to causes and contributing factors. Sometimes there are *indirect* causes and contributing factors. We read also of root causes, immediate causes, real causes, ultimate causes and main causes. What do all these words mean? How do we decide which causes to focus on? These questions must be addressed if we are to identify as systematically as possible the network or chains of causation which led to the accident. The book therefore adopts a particular definition of cause and uses it as consistently as possible.

This may lead to some surprises along the way about what is included as part of the causal network as well as what is excluded. One of the culminating points of the analysis in this book is the causal diagram in Chapter 10. As particular causes are discussed in the text, the interested reader may wish to refer to the diagram to see where they fit in the overall scheme.

Although networks of causation are theoretically infinite, interested parties focus on one or a small subset of factors when seeking to explain an accident. They may emphasise, for instance, operator error or, at the other end of the causal spectrum, the system of production for profit. Clearly there are principles of selection which people use, implicitly or explicitly, to guide their causal analysis. Where accident prevention is the issue, a principle implicitly used is to focus on causes which are controllable. Where questions of blame are involved the over-riding principle is to select causes which deflect blame to other parties.

Operator error

Operator error is frequently the first explanation provided for an accident. All too often, we hear that a rail accident occurred because the driver went through a red signal or that a plane crash was due to pilot error. But this is merely the starting point for analysis. As soon as we ask why the operator made the error in question we begin our journey back along the chains of causation. Operator error is actually one of the least useful causes to focus on since it is one of the least controllable. Operators will inevitably make errors sooner or later, if it is possible for them to do so. From a prevention point of view it is better to focus on factors further back along the causal chains which put operators in a position where it is possible for them to make critical errors.

Market forces and government regulation

When we extend the causal network far enough, market forces and cost cutting pressures are almost invariably implicated. Many accident investigations stop short of these factors, or at least do not include them systematically in the analysis. It is important to include them, however, since understanding how they operate may suggest ways of counteracting their effect. At the very least, including these factors explains the seeming inevitability of accidents. This book seeks to extend the causal analysis as widely as possible and stresses the role of government regulation in counteracting the tendency of market forces to push organisations towards accidents.

Organisational analysis

The report of the Royal Commission focused overwhelmingly on the technical causes of the explosion. Only one of its fifteen chapters was devoted to organisational causes – the chapter on management systems. This book adopts the reverse approach. It devotes as little attention as possible to the technical causes, and focuses on organisational or management system causes, on the principle that if we can get the organisational factors right the technical causes of accidents will not come into play. Moreover, the technical causes vary from one accident to another but the organisational failures which accident analyses reveal seem remarkably similar. A focus on organisational rather than technical causes therefore offers the best opportunity for generalisation, that is, the best opportunity for types of learning that can be transferred from one enterprise or industry to another.

High reliability organisations

Social scientists have recently been studying organisations which function with high reliability. At various points in this book, comparisons with high reliability organisations will be used to illuminate what went wrong at Longford. One of the central research findings is that high reliability organisations are characterised by a collective mindfulness about the possibility of disaster. Many of Esso's failures will turn out to be failures of mindfulness.

The Moura parallel

The similarities with the Moura disaster are so striking and the differences so instructive that comparisons will be made at appropriate points. (Readers should note the pronunciation of Moura: it rhymes with Now-ra.) But this book is not intended as a systematic comparison of the two disasters – it is Longford that is our focus of attention.

The structure of this book

The book is structured primarily as exploration of the causal network which generated the accident, starting with the most immediate causes and moving to the most remote. Chapter 2 examines the particular operator error which triggered the accident and initiates the search for more deep-seated causes. It introduces the concept of cause which is used throughout the book.

The next five chapters deal with a variety of organisational causes. Chapter 3 shows how Esso's failure to carry out appropriate hazard identification procedures contributed to the accident. Chapter 4 examines a practice which had developed at Longford of operating the plant outside the design limits. It shows how this practice had been allowed to develop because of inadequate oversight by Esso and that, in any case, the practice was sometimes necessary if Longford was to achieve its production targets. Chapter 5 looks at a variety of communication problems which contributed to the disaster, and in particular, the failure of Esso's incident reporting system. It makes suggestions about how good reporting systems can be designed. Chapter 6 looks at Esso's safety philosophy. It argues that using lost-time injury figures as a measure of safety, as Esso does, is inappropriate in hazardous industries, since it distracts attention from the management of major hazards. It shows, too, that Esso's emphasis on constructing a safety culture is highly problematic. Chapter 7 examines Esso's safety auditing and shows it to have been fundamentally flawed. It uses an audit carried out by BHP Coal, after the Moura explosion, to illustrate the kind of auditing required in hazardous industries. An audit carried out at Longford by the government agency, WorkCover, is also examined.

Chapter 8 moves beyond the organisation to the regulatory system. It concludes that the system of self-regulation in existence at Longford contributed to the accident and it advocates the "safety case" system, now in widespread use in Europe, as a way of regulating safety at sites where major hazards exist.

Chapter 9 moves to an even more remote causal level to investigate the claim that the privatisation of Victoria's gas distribution system contributed to the loss of supply experienced by Victorian consumers.

Chapter 10 presents a diagrammatic summary of the causal network identified in previous chapters. It then describes the claims about causation made in submissions to the Royal Commission and distils the principles which the participants used in selecting causes.

Chapter 11 draws the findings together. It shows how Esso's various failures can be summed up as an absence of mindfulness. It points out that mindfulness about the possibility of accidents involves not only searching within the organisation for warning signs, but also scanning the wider environment for lessons which can be learnt from organisations which have suffered major accidents. Esso was not good at heeding internal warnings nor at learning lessons from elsewhere. The chapter concludes by summarising the lessons which emerge from this analysis.

Research Note

This book relies heavily on the findings of the Royal Commission. But it is not simply a summary or a retelling of the story as presented in that report. I have reframed much of the material in terms of the general issues which arise in the literature on major accidents. Moreover, I have drawn extensively on the 6,500 pages of transcript testimony and on the submissions made to the inquiry by the parties represented. I have not provided page references to this material, but they are available on request from the author.

Chapter

2

Operator Error

Esso argued that control room operators and their supervisors on duty at the time made a number of crucial errors. But more than this, it claimed that the operators had been properly trained and there was therefore no excuse for their errors.

Esso's explanation for the accident was of course predictable. The company was facing claims totalling more than a billion dollars from gas customers who had been affected by the loss of supply. If it could argue that the accident was not its fault, but rather, the fault of some of its employees, it might escape liability. Moreover, if it could shift blame for the accident to the operators it would be able to defend itself against any prosecutions which the authorities might initiate.

While Esso clearly had a strong interest in arguing that operator error was the cause of the accident, its argument cannot be simply dismissed for this reason. In this chapter we shall explore the operator error explanation in some detail. We shall examine the actions of the operators and their immediate supervisors and the way in which these errors contributed to the accident. We shall find that although there were undoubtedly mistakes made by the operators, this is just the starting point for a proper understanding, not the total explanation which Esso claimed it was.

The input to the Longford gas plant is a mixture of gas, light hydrocarbon liquids and water which is piped ashore from Bass Strait. The components of the mixture are separated in a complex process of heating, cooling and pressure changes. From time to time variations in the mixture coming ashore can cause what are called "process upsets", that is disturbances in normal operating conditions. The morning of the accident, a severe process upset caused an automatic shutdown of the circulation of "lean" oil which warmed the plant. Operators did not manage to restart the circulation for some hours. This caused a 14-tonne metal heat exchanger to become extremely cold – about 50 degrees below zero.

The operators and their supervisors then made a critical error – they decided to reintroduce the warm oil into the heat exchanger after it had become super cold. A cold glass is likely to shatter if boiling water is poured into it; metal which has been chilled to a low enough temperature becomes brittle and can be expected to fracture in much the same way, if suddenly warmed. This is exactly what happened on the day of the accident – the cold, brittle metal fractured in a catastrophic way, allowing vast quantities of gas and volatile liquid to escape, find an ignition point and catch fire. The company claimed that operators had been trained about the dangers of cold temperature embrittlement and should have known better. They should have allowed the heat exchanger to thaw out before they began to re-establish the warm liquid flow.

Let us examine Esso's claim in a little more detail. They claimed that inexcusable failures by operators occurred at several points in the accident sequence. First, operators could and should have prevented the process upset from developing to the point that the warm oil system shut down. (I shall deal with this issue extensively in a later chapter.) Second, operators should have known that the warm oil system needed to be restarted as a matter of urgency; and third, given that they failed to restart the system quickly, which allowed the heater exchangers to become super cold, they should have known about the dangers of then reintroducing warm oil. The operator on duty at the time was singled out to bear the brunt of the blame. According to Esso even though he knew it was his job to attend to the process upset, he ignored it. Moreover, once the warm oil circulation had stopped the same man failed to apply himself as a matter of urgency to restarting the circulation. Finally, after the heat exchanger had become super cold, he participated with others in the fatal decision to restart the warm oil flow. The Esso submission claims that the operator "was in possession of the necessary information" and failed to take appropriate action "due to reasons peculiar to himself".

At one point in the proceedings Esso produced an overseas expert witness to support its attack upon the operators. This witness noted that although the operators had said they did not understand the consequences of very cold temperatures, they had all been trained, and their evidence to the Commission was not to be believed. A little later this same expert elaborated on why the operators might have denied that they knew about the dangers of very cold temperatures:

It might be so because the operators today have very strong and very deep emotions about what happened out there and they have completely blocked certain things from their minds so that they can go ahead and sleep at night.

Esso's submission to the Royal Commission blaming the operators and singling out one for particular criticism provoked an angry reaction from the union, whose members immediately went on strike, again threatening Victoria's gas supply. However, the State Premier (Kennett) managed to retrieve the situation by publicly expressing the view that Esso's submission was stupid and that it assassinated the character of one of the workers. He urged the men back to work, saying that "two wrongs don't make a right" (*The Age*, 28/4/99). This was an extraordinarily conciliatory response from an anti-union premier, demonstrating yet again just how politically sensitive the matter was.

Problems with the theory of operator error

The theory of operator error is not just a device for protecting the interests of companies which suffer major accidents; it is a widely adopted style of explanation. It accords with common-sense understandings of causation in terms of the actions or inactions of individuals, and many accident investigations come to an end once they have identified individuals who can be held responsible.

Sophisticated accident analysts, however, consistently resist this style of explanation, for at least two reasons. First, it is often unjust, and second, it generates very few insights into how accidents may be prevented. I shall develop these ideas in the next sections before returning to the Longford operators.

The TMI nuclear power station accident

One analyst who stressed the unfairness of the operator error explanation was Charles Perrow, who developed his ideas in the process of analysing the accident at the Three Mile Island nuclear power station near New York in 1979. This accident, which by good fortune injured no one, very nearly ended in a nuclear meltdown which could have affected millions. Because of its potential consequences, the accident was investigated by a high-powered Presidential Commission, which identified operator error as the major cause of the accident (Perrow, 1982:177).

Perrow's principal argument against the thesis of operator error is that the situation confronting the operators at Three Mile Island was so complex and opaque that they could not possibly be expected to understand what was happening or what actions they should take to deal with the problem. In order to make this argument Perrow developed a theory of what he called Normal Accidents. He argued that technologies such as those involved in nuclear power production are so complex and so tightly coupled (in the sense that things follow one after another in rapid succession) that accidents are inevitable. In such contexts accidents are beyond the capacity of operators to prevent. He noted that as the accident sequence develops, "for some critical time period the nature of the accident is incomprehensible to those seeking to control it" (Perrow, 1982:174).

Perrow's theory that accidents are normal and inevitable in certain high technology systems is hardly very useful from an accident prevention point of view. Its value lies in highlighting the unfairness in these circumstances of blaming the "hapless operators", as he calls them – of regarding them as the "villains of the piece" (Perrow, 1984:24), as so often happens.

But what is the relevance of this to the Longford accident? Perrow (1984:chap 4) claims that the kind of technology he identified in the nuclear power industry is also to be found in petrochemical plants. It is perhaps not surprising, then, that there are similarities between the accidents at Three Mile Island (TMI) and at Longford. Consider this.

TMI suffered an accident in which the liquid which normally cooled the reactor core began to drain away. This was the equivalent of the process upset at Longford. An automatic safety device at TMI switched on pumps to inject water into the reactor core to prevent it from overheating. Operators did not fully understand what was happening and switched off the water injection pumps; this was the critical error which led to the near meltdown. At Longford, the process upset led ultimately to the automatic shut down of the warm oil pumps. Operators did not fully understand what was going on and eventually started the warm oil flow again; this was the critical error which led to the fracturing of the heat exchanger and the subsequent explosion. This way of construing it is, of course, a substantial simplification of what happened, in both cases, but it does serve to bring out the essential similarity of the two accident sequences.

I have jumped ahead a little by assuming here that the operators at Longford did not fully understand the situation they were in, but if, when we examine their role more closely, this turns out to be a fair assumption, we shall be justified in concluding that the hapless Longford operators were no more culpable than those at TMI.

Active failures and latent conditions

The second reason for resisting operator error as a complete explanation is that it is not helpful from an accident prevention point of view. Human beings inevitably make errors and errors by operators must be expected. Thus, rather than focusing on the operators who make the errors, modern accident analysis looks for the conditions which made the errors possible. It is nearly always the case that there was a whole series of contributory factors which created an operator error and set up the situation which made the error critical. Accident analyses which aim to prevent a recurrence seek to identify these factors. From this perspective errors are seen as consequences rather than principal causes (Reason, 1997:10).

Reason has developed this idea by distinguishing between *active failures* and *latent conditions* as follows:

> [**Active failures** are the] *errors and violations committed at the 'sharp end' of the system – by pilots, air traffic controllers, police officers, insurance brokers, financial traders, ships' crews,*

control room operators, maintenance personnel and the like. Such unsafe acts are likely to have a direct impact on the safety of the system ...

Latent conditions *are to technological organisations what resident pathogens are to the human body. Like pathogens, latent conditions – such as poor design, gaps in supervision, undetected manufacturing defects or maintenance failures, unworkable procedures, clumsy automation, shortfalls in training, less than adequate tools and equipment – may be present for many years before they combine with local circumstances and active failures to penetrate the system's many layers of defences. They arise from strategic and other top-level decisions made by governments, regulators, manufacturers, designers and organisational managers. The impact of these decisions spreads throughout the organisation, shaping a distinctive corporate culture and creating error-producing factors within the individual workplaces.*

Note that while this analysis acknowledges that many major accidents may be triggered by operators, it identifies latent conditions as the cause of such errors. Reason argues that if major accidents are to be prevented, attention must be paid to the latent conditions which give rise to critical errors by front line operators.

Reason also points out that not all major accidents are triggered by active failures. In some cases latent failures lead directly to disaster when certain local circumstances occur, without any error by front line operators. For example, the Moura disaster was caused by management failure to monitor and react to changes in the mine atmosphere which meant that coal smouldering in a remote part of the mine went undetected until it ignited a methane gas explosion. Front line operators (miners) did not contribute in any way to this event, although eleven of them died. Moura was a time bomb set by management and triggered by the passage of time, not by the miners. The theory of latent errors is thus more widely applicable than any simple theory of operator error.

Reason's insight about the causal significance of latent conditions is now widely understood by professional accident analysts, although the language used to express it varies. Sometimes the point is made by saying that accidents result from failures in the organisation's safety management system, which need to be addressed if further accidents are to be prevented. Alternatively, some writers stress the importance of identifying the "root causes" of an accident.

When is a cause a "root cause"?

The concept of root cause analysis raises an interesting question: how far back along the causal chain do we go before we are satisfied that we have identified the root causes? Should we be satisfied with some of the latent conditions identified by Reason such as gaps in supervision or inadequate maintenance procedures, which come under the general heading of management system failure? Should we go further back and identify government policies such as de-regulation as the root cause? Or should we go even further back and nominate a system of production which is driven by profit above all else as the ultimate explanation? Where should we stop in our quest for causes? Clearly we need what Rasmussen (1990) has called *stop rules*.

Blaming the operator implicitly assumes the stop rule that once we have identified a deliberate unsafe act or violation by an operator we can stop our inquiry. This was Esso's stop rule. On Esso's view the operators knew what they should have done and, for reasons best known to themselves, didn't do it. The company was not concerned to ask what those reasons were since, according to its stop rule, the explanation was complete.

At the other end of the causal chain it is at least plausible to argue that production for profit generates pressures which inevitably compromise safety. Every thorough analysis of a major accident produces evidence of the way in which cost considerations contributed to the accident (Glasbeek and Tucker, 1993; Carson, 1982; Hopkins, 1999). But the problem with following the causal chain back to production or cost pressures is that, realistically, such pressures must be regarded as a given, at least in the short term. There is nothing much that can be done about this particular root cause unless and until society as a whole is willing to reorder its priorities. While this may ultimately be the most effective way to prevent major accidents it does not give much guidance in the here and now.

This last point suggests one stop rule which we might apply in carrying out root cause analysis. Stop when the causes identified are no longer controllable (Reason, 1997:236). An interesting feature of this rule is that it suggests different stopping points for different parties. For companies, it makes sense to trace causes back to management system failures; these are the root controllable causes. For governments, on the other hand, it makes sense to go one step further and ask whether a failure of the regulatory system was the root cause, for this is a matter which governments can do something about.

Operator training

The preceding discussion provides compelling reasons for going beyond operator error as an explanation of the Longford accident. But in order to do so we must further examine Esso's claim that the operators had been taught the danger of very cold temperature and the operators' counter claim that they did not understand this danger. What are we to make of these contrasting claims?

There was ample evidence given at the inquiry that the operators did not appreciate the situation they were in. This is strikingly illustrated by the focus of their attention following the failure of the warm oil flow. Some time after the cessation of this flow, another heat exchanger (not the one which eventually fractured) began to leak, and hundreds, if not thousands, of litres of liquid flowed onto the ground. When metal is cooled it contracts or shrinks, and metal joints which are normally well sealed may no longer fit snugly, leaving gaps through which a contained liquid can escape. The leak was caused in this way by the very low temperatures in the heat exchanger, but this was not initially understood by operators who assumed that bolts on the vessel might have been incorrectly tensioned. Maintenance men were called to re-tension the bolts but they eventually found that no adjustment was needed. The fact is that the leak was merely a symptom of a more fundamental problem, and the proposed solution – retensioning the bolts – revealed the operators' lack of understanding of what was happening (Dawson, 3.58). As counsel assisting put it, it was the operators' "lack of knowledge which caused them to be distracted by the leak in [the heat exchanger] in the hours between the loss of lean oil flow and the incident".

But although there is no doubt that operators did not understand the dangers of cold metal embrittlement, it is also true that they had been trained about it, as Esso claimed. How can this be? We explore this paradox in what follows.

Operators were classified as Tech 1 or Tech 2 and paid accordingly. In order to achieve these classifications they had to study for and pass tests conducted by Esso's training supervisor. The tests related to a series of training modules which covered aspects of the operation of the gas plant. Answers to the tests were in writing. Correct answers were ticked; incorrect were marked – "training required". Answers which were nearly correct were marked "coaching required". In such cases, the assessor took the candidate to the relevant section of the plant and explained the situation. The candidate was then asked if he understood. If the answer was yes the item was ticked off. If the answer was no, the matter was re-explained. According to one of the operators who gave evidence at the inquiry, it took "gumption" to ask for a re-explanation. It is a reasonable inference, therefore, that operators did not always fully understand the matters about which they had been coached.

This inference is borne out by evidence given at the Commission, where the written test results of one operator were examined. Several of the answers indicated that the operator had needed coaching. But when the operator was shown his answers at the Commission, he still could not see what was wrong with them, despite the fact that he had been coached about his mistakes. Clearly, this coaching process was far from adequate.

For example, one of the critical test items asked what happened if the pumps maintaining the warm oil flow shut down and were not restarted urgently. The operator's answer made no mention of the dangers of cold temperatures and the answer was marked as indicating a need for coaching. At the Commission hearings the operator still did not know what was wrong with his answer.

Another question asked why it was that a certain valve closed off a flow of liquid in one part of the plant when the temperature of the liquid dropped below a certain point. The operator's answer was that the purpose was to prevent any "thermal damage" to downstream pipe work. This was the correct answer and he received a tick. He was asked at the Commission what he meant by "thermal damage". He replied that he "had no concept of what that meant". Thermal damage was the answer contained in the training documents and he understood that this was the answer required in order to get the necessary tick. Counsel for Esso at the inquiry pushed him on what the term, "thermal damage", might have meant to him at the time, and the image which came to his mind was "some form of pipe work deformity", or alternatively, "ice hitting something and damaging pipe work". This operator had no idea at the time that the thermal damage referred to was the fact that metals at low enough temperature become brittle and hence are likely to shatter if suddenly warmed.

Counsel for Esso tried hard to suggest at the inquiry that the operator had shown a lack of integrity in providing the answer he knew was required without having a clear idea of what that answer meant. "So you were prepared to go on and accept a position as a Tech 2 without knowing what you meant by an answer that actually gave you that qualification?", counsel asked. The operator responded that this was "normal practice among all operators".

But there is nothing reprehensible about the operator's behaviour in this respect. People regularly pass exams without getting full marks, that is, without complete knowledge of their subject matter, but nevertheless go out to practice their new profession, knowing that their knowledge is incomplete. The presumption is that learning continues on the job.

The incomplete knowledge of the operators to which counsel for Esso drew attention cannot reasonably be blamed on the operators; it is clearly a consequence of the training process itself. Esso's training was a form of competency-based training – as it turns out, a rather degenerate form. It identified the specific knowledge which operators required to do their job, provided them with this information and tested whether they could present this information back to an assessor. It did not test for understanding. An alternative approach would aim to provide an understanding of the fundamental scientific or engineering principles involved. Such an approach would give operators considerably more knowledge than was required for routine plant operations, but would make them better able to analyse and deal with non-routine occurrences (Kletz, 1994:235). This alternative might be described as education rather than training. It culminates in a science or engineering degree rather than a certificate of competency. What I am suggesting, then, is that the operators' inadequate understanding of the danger they were in is in part a result of the minimalist and degenerate form of competency-based training they had received and highlights the importance of a professional education. The need for engineering expertise on site at Longford is a matter I shall deal with at greater length in a later chapter, but to foreshadow that discussion here, the safe operation of a hazardous plant like Longford requires engineering expertise, not merely competency-based training.

I am not suggesting that engineers would automatically have understood the dangers of loss of warm oil flow. The Longford plant manager, who happened to be absent on the day of the accident, was himself an engineer, yet he:

> *did not know that the loss of lean oil circulation would result in the plant getting colder, nor did he know of the dangers of cold metal embrittlement. The fact that the lean oil flow had stopped for some hours would not have "rung a specific alarm bell"* (Dawson, 13.27).

The plant manger reported to an operations manager located at Esso's Melbourne office. Even this man, also an engineer who had formerly been in charge at Longford, said that he had no idea before the accident that a loss of lean oil flow for any length of time would be a hazard (Dawson, 13.28).

As I shall argue later, only engineers with an intimate familiarity with the day-to-day operations of the plant might have been expected to understand the hazardous nature of the situation. There were no such engineers at Longford.

The fact is that the failure to recognise the danger of embrittlement was widespread in Esso. Not only were the operators and their immediate supervisors unaware of the problem, but so also were their senior managers. Given these circumstances it is hardly enlightening to attribute the accident to operator error.

The "real" causes

The report of the Royal Commission made a distinction between "immediate" and "real" causes. Immediate causes referred to the sequence of technical events, starting with the process upset, which culminated in the rupture of the heat exchanger and the escape of inflammable gas. But the report identified the real causes as the inadequate knowledge and training of the operators which prevented them from taking appropriate preventive action as the accident sequence developed. The Commission noted that:

> *the lack of knowledge on the part of both the operators and supervisors was directly attributable to a deficiency in their initial and subsequent training. Not only was their training inadequate, but there were no current operating procedures to guide them in dealing with the problem which they encountered* ... (Dawson, 15.6).

In identifying the "real causes" in this way, the Commission was very firmly rejecting any suggestion that the operators were to blame. Without explicitly saying so, it was rejecting Esso's submission that operator error provided a complete explanation for the accident. It was also rejecting Esso's implicit stop rule that the quest for causes can be terminated once errors by front line operators have been identified.

But the Commission did not define its concept of real cause, and its use of this term suggested that inadequate knowledge and training constituted a complete explanation. It suggested, in other words, that the quest for causal understanding could stop at this point. That, at any rate, was how the Commission's words were understood in the press. *The Age* reported the Commission as finding that "inadequate training of staff was the *ultimate cause* of the fatal explosion" (29/6/99:8), while *The Canberra Times* reported that "the *main cause* was found to be a lack of staff training" (29/6/99:4, emphasis added).

Inquiries into major accidents often seem satisfied to identify training and information deficiencies as root causes, leading to recommendations about further training as the remedy. But there is no logical reason to stop the inquiry at this point. Although the Commission spoke of inadequate information and training as the "real causes", we are entitled to ask: "Why was the training so inadequate?" and "Why were the operators and their managers so ignorant of the dangers?". As soon as we ask these questions, a host of other contributory factors comes into view. These factors are further back along the causal chain and, in this sense, more fundamental. We need to uncover these more fundamental causes in order to identify the more fundamental failures of Longford.

Causation in law

There is something of a puzzle here. The Commission was well aware of a range of contributory factors and drew various conclusions about their significance. But it stopped short of describing them as "real causes". Why did it limit itself in this way? What kind of stop rule was it operating with?

To answer this question we must begin by distinguishing between "causation in law" and non-legal conceptions of causation (see Brooks, 1988:74). In common usage, anything about which we can make a "but for" statement can count as a cause. For instance, it might be said that *but for* operator error this accident would not have occurred; *but for* faulty operating instructions, a faulty safety management system, an inadequate regulatory system etc., this accident would not have occurred. Had any of these matters been otherwise, the accident would not have occurred. It is clear that "but for" factors can be very remote from an event and still count as a cause.

We should note at this point that the number of causes in the "but for" sense is potentially infinite. For instance, suppose I have an accident at work. The very fact that I came to work is a cause in the sense that had I not come to work I would not have been injured. In most circumstances, however, it would not be regarded as useful to identify my decision to come to work as a cause, since identifying this causal connection would normally be of no practical significance. Here, therefore, is a stop rule with which we implicitly operate in normal discourse: stop when the cause in question is of no practical significance.

Interestingly, there are contexts in which this eminently sensible rule is not observed. Grieving relatives of someone killed in an air crash may sometimes think or even say: "if only she had not made the last minute decision to travel on that particular flight, she would not have been killed". In making this causal connection they are ignoring the stop rule identified above.

Consider now the question of causation in law. For lawyers, causation is often closely associated with allocating blame, that is, identifying legal liability – liability to pay damages or liability for punishment. From this perspective causation is equivalent to legal liability (Mason, 1991; Brooks, 1988:74-7 offers a powerful critique of this view). The implicit stop rule here is: stop when causal analysis is no longer of assistance in attributing legal liability. For instance, while it might be argued the ultimate cause of an industrial accident is the system of production for profit, there is no way legal liability for such an accident can be attributed to the capitalist system. Similarly, the limitations of the government's regulatory framework do not give rise to any legal liability for a specific accident, even though it may be possible to argue that, *but for* certain deficiencies in the regulatory regime, the accident would probably not have occurred. Part of the reason why such factors do not give rise to liability is that they are too remote from the event in question (see Freckelton, 1997). If one is interested in identifying parties who are sufficiently culpable that they can be made to pay (either damages or a penalty) then one cannot proceed very far back along the causal chain before attributions of blame appear unreasonable and liability peters out.

It seems, therefore, that in restricting the notion of cause in the way it did the Commission was adopting the stop rules of the legal profession rather than those relevant to an accident prevention framework. Fortunately, the Commission went well beyond "causation in law" by identifying "contributing factors" as well as causes. Its analysis was therefore in no way limited by its conceptual framework and its findings about contributing factors are relevant for accident prevention purposes. But understanding the Commission's concept of cause provides some insight into the otherwise strangely limited conclusion it comes to about "real causes".

Conclusion

The catastrophic failure of the heat exchanger was triggered by operator error. In fact several staff at Longford participated in the faulty decision to re-warm the metal heat exchanger which had become brittle with cold. But in no sense can these men be blamed for their decision since not even their senior managers understood the danger inherent in the situation. The fact is that none of the men concerned had been properly trained about the dangers of cold metal embrittlement and the company had not developed procedures to deal with this danger. Operator error has proved to be an unsatisfactory explanation here, just as it has in so many other major accident investigations.

Nor is it sufficient to explain what happened in terms of inadequate training. There are more deep-seated reasons for this training failure. These root causes or latent conditions (to use Reason's term) will be explored in later chapters, generating a number of important lessons which are relevant to high hazard industries in general.

Chapter

3

The Failure to Identify Hazards

Identifying inadequate training of the operators as the cause of the accident, as the Royal Commission did, immediately provokes further questions: why was their training so inadequate and why were the operators and their managers so ignorant of the dangers they faced? The basic answer is that the company had failed to identify the relevant hazards and therefore to take steps to deal with them. This chapter explores some of the reasons for the failure to identify hazards which contributed to the accident.

Managing safety in any enterprise, large or small, starts with hazard identification. This is a fundamental principle. Elaborate safety management systems are not a prerequisite and, as Berger (1999a) makes clear, anyone can play spot-the-hazard. NSW WorkCover captures this essential simplicity in its guide to basic risk management for small and medium businesses (Hazpak):

Imagine that a ten-year-old child were to be brought into your workplace. What would you warn them to be extra careful about?

Esso has introduced its workforce to this idea with its strategy of "stepback five by five". This requires workers to step back five paces (metaphorically) and invest five minutes to think about "things to watch out for" before they start work on any particular job. (Smith,

1997). They do this individually for single jobs and, where the task is collective, in groups led by a supervisor.

Of course not all hazards are obvious and firms using complex technologies will need to adopt systematic means to seek them out. But, as one expert on loss control has put it: "once the [hazards] have been identified, the battle is more than half won" (see Dawson, 13.49).

The point was well understood by Esso's parent company Exxon. An Exxon safety review noted that:

> *To prevent the undesirable consequences of accidents, one must first identify the hazards which can lead to accidents. Once the hazards have been identified, a major stumbling block to loss or accident prevention has been overcome* (see Dawson, 13.50).

This is not only the common-sense approach; it is also the law. All modern legislation requires employers first to identify and then to assess and control hazards at work. Of particular relevance to Esso's case is the Victorian *Occupational Health and Safety (Plant) Regulations 1995* which require employers "to ensure all hazards associated with the installation, commissioning, erection and use of plant and systems of work associated with that plant are identified". Even the most sophisticated regulatory approach, the safety case regime to be discussed in a later chapter, starts with this requirement that hazards be identified.

HAZOP

The standard hazard identification process in the petrochemical industry is the "hazard and operability" study, or HAZOP for short. A HAZOP involves systematically imagining everything that might go wrong in a processing plant and developing procedures or engineering solutions to avoid these potential problems. It uses a "what if?" methodology, that is it asks a series of "what if" questions: What will happen if the temperature at this point is too high? too low? the pressure is too high? too low? the flow ceases because of pump failure? and so on. Bahr (1997:110) describes the process as follows:

> *A team of engineers methodically analyses a system and through the use of guide words, asks how the process could deviate from its intended operation and what the effects would be. The group divides the system into nodes (points or junctions) and using the*

pre-established guide words (no flow, less flow, high temperature etc), ponders the questions of what could occur if the process deviated in some fashion. In other words a HAZOP is a somewhat controlled technical brainstorming session.

HAZOP studies became a standard technique in industries such as oil refining and gas processing in the mid-1980s and from about that time Exxon required its affiliates to carry out such studies as part of the design process for all new plant. In the case of existing plant, retrospective HAZOPs were to be carried out as needed.

Exxon was particularly concerned about the issue of cold temperature embrittlement and the possibility of catastrophic failure of metal parts exposed to temperatures lower than they were designed for. Accordingly, Esso's guidelines warned HAZOP study teams to pay special attention to this matter.

Esso operated more than one gas plant at Longford. There were in fact three interconnected gas plants and another facility known as a crude oil stabilisation plant. Gas plant 1, where the accident occurred, was the oldest, built in 1969. Gas plants 2 and 3 were built later. Esso had carried out retrospective HAZOPs in 1994 and 1995 of all these facilities, *except* gas plant 1.

A HAZOP for gas plant 1 was planned for 1995 and the cost of the study was included in Esso's budget for that year. The figure budgeted was $70,000, a modest sum by industry standards. But the planned study never took place. Although no formal decisions were taken it seems that each year the matter was simply deferred. One reason given for this indefinite deferral was that the study would have "picked up too many little items". Why this was a problem was never explained. It will be remembered that once hazards are identified they must then be assessed for their significance. If they are judged not to represent a significant risk they can be assigned a low priority. Merely identifying a hazard does not commit a company to taking action. To fail to carry out a hazard identification process for fear that it might identify too many hazards is, to say the least, bizarre. The deferral in 1995 was also explained as a matter of resources. It was said that the resources required for the HAZOP could be put to better use attending to issues thrown up in another risk assessment exercise undertaken in 1994. It was not explained, however, why this required deferment year after year.

One hint as to why Esso seemed so unconcerned about conducting the HAZOP on gas plant 1 was provided by one of its consultants. This man was asked whether an efficient and astute operator would want to review older plant from time to time to gauge the extent to which it departed from modern standards. His reply was that the general principle was – "if it ain't broke, don't fix it". He noted that this had applied to gas plant 1 in that it had operated for nearly 30 years without a problem. This view is completely at odds with the philosophy of safety management in relation to rare but catastrophic events. The fact that a major accident has not happened in the past provides no guarantee for the future. But illogical though this witness's position may be, it does provide some insight into the kind of thinking which may have led to the indefinite deferment of the HAZOP of gas plant 1.

Did the lack of a HAZOP contribute to the accident?

The question of whether the failure to carry out a HAZOP of gas plant 1 contributed to the accident was a central issue at the inquiry. The Commission came to the view that the failure to conduct the HAZOP indeed contributed to the explosion. It found that it was "inconceivable" that such a study would have failed to pinpoint the fact that a loss of warm oil flow could lead to dangerously low temperatures and the possibility of brittle fracture (Dawson, 13.55). Such a discovery would have led Esso to develop protective control systems and procedures to deal with the loss of warm oil flow. These would have included instructions to terminate the cold liquid flows, and written procedures for restarting equipment which had become super cold.

It is interesting to note that an Exxon investigative team which arrived in Australia immediately after the accident initially concurred with this finding. A document prepared in connection with its investigation concluded that "the lack of a detailed HAZOP for gas plant 1 is considered a contributing factor to this incident" (Dawson, 13.56). The final version of the team's report did not contain this statement and Esso provided no evidence to explain this omission. It should be noted here that if the failure to conduct the HAZOP were to be accepted by the courts as a contributory factor, it would be more difficult for Esso to escape liability by claiming that the accident was purely and simply a consequence of operator error. The initial finding was therefore not in the company's interest. The earlier draft document came to light only because the Victorian authorities had seized various documents and critical equipment shortly after the fire in order to prevent evidence from being tampered with or disappearing.

An interactive, multiple failure

During the inquiry Esso did produce an argument as to why the HAZOP could not have been expected to prevent the accident. It is worth examining here because of its wider implications.

The accident sequence, starting with the process upset the previous night, was long and complex and numerous factors contributed to it along the way. For reasons to be discussed in later chapters, operators ignored various alarms and failed to take effective action to control the upset. The upset led eventually, by a causal sequence which was not entirely clear, even in retrospect, to an automatic shutdown of the warm oil pumps. The operators were then unable to restart the pumps which meant that the heat exchangers became steadily colder. Finally, after it was too late to safely restart the pumps, they got them going and reintroduced warm oil into the heat exchanger causing catastrophic brittle fracture.

This complexity led one Esso witness to describe the sequence of events as an "interactive, multiple failure scenario". He noted that "HAZOP methodology has an inherent weakness that precludes the identification of interactive, multiple failure scenarios", that weakness being that it can deal with only one thing at a time. He went on to observe that it had "taken five months of intensive investigation to fully identify and understand the contributing factors that led to the incident ... The likelihood that a HAZOP would have found this multi-faceted scenario is, at best, remote." Counsel for Esso picked up this theme, arguing that a HAZOP "would be unlikely to identify the combination of problems giving rise to the failure of [the heat exchanger]".

This is not the first time this kind of argument has been used to account for major accidents. Charles Perrow provides a remarkably similar analysis in his account of the accident at the Three Mile Island nuclear power station. He describes that accident as a normal or system accident: it is normal in the sense of inevitable in certain high technology industries such as nuclear power generation and petrochemical processing; and it is a system accident in that it involves more than just the failure of a single critical component. "A normal accident occurs", he says, "... when there are unanticipated multiple failures in the equipment, design, or operator actions". The last step in his argument is that the precise configuration of events in any normal accident is so complex that the accident sequence cannot be anticipated and is therefore unpreventable. "The normal accident cannot be prevented because it is not possible to create faultless systems" (Perrow, 1982:174,176).

There is, however, a crucial logical flaw in this final step. It is true that accidents like Three Mile Island and Longford, which involve interactive, multiple failures, are extraordinarily complex and that the precise accident sequences are almost unimaginable in advance, and certainly unpredictable. But it is not necessary to predict the entire accident sequence in order to be able to avoid it. The fact is that had any one of the errors or malfunctions in a system accident not occurred, the accident would not have occurred. The accident sequence is actually highly susceptible to interruption. Though unpredictable, it is entirely preventable.

In the Longford case it was not necessary to foresee the entire series of failures in order to prevent the accident. A HAZOP would have identified the last link in the chain of events, namely, that a loss of warm oil might lead to cold temperature embrittlement of the heat exchanger. This danger would then have been controlled. Thus, even though the accident sequence might have begun because of other problems which had not been foreseen or controlled, it would have been terminated at this point.

This was the position taken by the Royal Commission. Its conclusion was that "*notwithstanding* [the technical complexity of the accident sequence] ... the conclusion is inevitable that the accident which occurred on 25 September 1998 would not have occurred had appropriate steps been taken following the tripping of the [warm oil] pumps" (Dawson, 15.6, emphasis added).

It is clear, therefore, that Esso's claim that the HAZOP methodology is flawed because it cannot encompass an entire accident sequence is misguided. In the circumstances it looks like little more than an attempt to minimise the significance of the company's failure to carry out the planned HAZOP in order to minimise its legal liability.

The absence of procedures

As noted above the Commission's view was that a HAZOP would have identified the need for written procedures for dealing with the loss of warm oil flow, as well as procedures for plant shutdown and restart which occur infrequently and may present special dangers not faced during normal plant operation. The absence of start up and shutdown procedures was contrary to Exxon policy and Esso management could provide no explanation to the Commission for their failure to comply with the parent company requirements in this respect. The Commission concluded that "the lack of proper operating procedures, therefore, contributed to the occurrence" (Dawson, p236).

This provides a context for the Commission's earlier mentioned conclusion about inadequate training as a real cause. The training which would have helped operators avert the accident was training in correct procedures for dealing with loss of warm oil flow. But there were no such procedures. The lack of training is therefore a symptom of the problem rather than a satisfactory explanation. As suggested in the previous chapter, to identify lack of training as the cause raises more questions than it answers.

At this point it may be useful, by way of summary, to spell out the causal chain which is implicit in the preceding discussion. An immediate cause of the accident was the lack of operator training on how to handle the failure of warm oil flow. This in turn was a consequence of the lack of appropriate procedures in which operators might have been trained. The absence of procedures stemmed from the failure of the company to carry out the relevant HAZOP. And the failure to conduct the HAZOP was attributable to concern about resources. Where the emphasis is placed depends on one's purposes, but in the context of this chapter, it is the failure to conduct a HAZOP which constitutes the root cause.

The hazards of interconnectedness

One accident which is deeply etched in the minds of people in the petroleum industry is the Piper Alpha oil platform fire in the North Sea off the coast of Scotland in 1988 in which 167 men lost their lives. The

Longford operator who activated the emergency shutdown system after the explosion told the inquiry that his intention was to avoid "another Piper Alpha".

One of factors which contributed to the fire on Piper Alpha was the connection to adjacent platforms. Product from these platforms was pumped ashore *via* Piper Alpha. This meant that gas from other platforms fuelled the conflagration, intensifying and prolonging it.

Longford's gas plant 1 was connected to the two other gas plants and the crude oil stabilisation plant. There was thus a possibility, at least in principle, that a fire at any one of these plants might be fed by oil or gas from another. In this respect the dangers of interconnectedness at Longford were strikingly similar to the dangers of interconnectedness on Piper Alpha.

One of the obvious lessons from Piper Alpha for Esso, then, concerned the importance of being able to isolate plant quickly and effectively. But this was not a matter Esso attended to. The emergency shutdown procedure did not effectively isolate gas plant 1. The heat from the fire ruptured nearby piping which connected gas plant 1 with the other plants. This meant that far more inventory (oil and gas) was available to fuel the fire. In the end it was 53 hours before operators finally managed to isolate the fuel that was feeding the fire.

Gas plants 2 and 3 were not damaged in the fire but before they could be restarted they had to be totally isolated from gas plant 1. There were numerous interconnecting pipes and, as the Commission observed, "to identify all of the isolation points that would be required to effect a safe restart ... was a complex task which involved an intimate knowledge of the plant" (Dawson, 9.4). It took an Esso team more than a week to identify these points and carry out the necessary work. As it turned out, 85 isolations were necessary to ensure that gas plant 1 was completely cut off from gas plants 2 and 3 (Dawson, 9.4). Thus, not only did the interconnectedness of the gas plants at Longford contribute to the intensity of the fire, but in the words of counsel assisting the Commission, "the interconnection certainly contributed to the delay in isolating gas plants 2 and 3 for restart".

Gas plants 2 and 3 were built after gas plant 1. However no study was done at the time they were built to identify the hazards which might result from the interconnection of these plants and the ways in which this might threaten the supply of gas to Victoria. According to counsel assisting, a properly designed hazard identification process "would almost inevitably have identified the risk of interruption of supply". Nor was any detailed consideration given to just what steps would be needed to achieve complete isolation in the event of fire. The Piper Alpha disaster occurred after the completion of gas plants 2 and 3, but there is no evidence that the dangers of interconnectedness at Longford were re-examined in the light of that event.

The hazards of change

Processing plants evolve and grow over time. A study of petroleum refineries in the US has shown that "the largest and most complex refineries in the sample are also the oldest ... Their complexity emerged as a result of historical accretion. Processes were modified, added, linked, enhanced and replaced over a history that greatly exceeded the memories of those who worked in the refinery" (quoted in Perrow, 1999:364). Such modifications inevitably introduce new hazards, and pessimists conclude that accidents are inevitable in such contexts (Perrow, 1999). However, those who are committed to accident prevention draw a different conclusion, namely, that it is important that every time physical changes are made to plant these changes be subjected to a systematic hazard identification process.

Esso's own management of change philosophy recognises this. It notes that "changes potentially invalidate prior risk assessments and can create new risks, if not managed diligently" (Dawson, 13.65). But Esso did not live up to its own standards in this regard: gas plants 2 and 3 were added to the Longford site without any consideration of the risks of interconnectedness.

There were two other management of change failures which contributed to the accident which I mention here because they will be relevant in later chapters. Part of the mixture entering gas plant 1 was a light hydrocarbon liquid known as condensate. This liquid must be separated and specially treated. In 1992 a pipeline was installed to transfer excess quantities of condensate from gas plant 1 to gas plant 2 and in subsequent years further modifications were made to this system to improve the efficiency of the production process. But the transfer of condensate required certain parts of gas plant 1 to be operated at lower than design temperature (Dawson, 13.78) and this contributed to the process upset which initiated the accident sequence in ways which will be discussed in a later chapter. The point to be made here, however, is that this series of changes was made without a proper assessment of the risks involved. The Commission notes that "as a consequence, for some time before the accident ... operators were transferring condensate ... without a full understanding of the potential hazards associated with the process" (Dawson, 13.75).

A second relevant change was the relocation to Melbourne in 1992 of all the engineering staff who had previously worked at Longford, leaving the Longford operators without the engineering backup to which they were accustomed. Following their removal from Longford, engineers were expected to monitor the plant from a distance and operators were expected to telephone the engineers when they felt a need to. Perhaps predictably, these arrangements did not work effectively, and I shall argue in the next chapter that the absence of engineering expertise had certain long-term consequences which contributed to the accident. It is worth emphasising also, as the Commission did (Dawson, 13.83), that as a result of this change there were no engineers on site on the day of the accident and it was left entirely to the operators and their immediate supervisors to deal with the crisis.

Esso did not systematically attempt to identify the hazards involved in relocating its on-site engineers. Management of change guidelines usually cover "human resourcing" changes (eg DPIE, 1995:82) and Esso's own management of change philosophy specifies that the changes to be managed include "changes to personnel and organisation". It follows that this is yet another area where the company failed to measure up to its own standards.

Exxon's hands-off approach

Esso's numerous failures raise the question of the role of the parent company, Exxon, in ensuring that hazards are properly identified. Exxon promulgated a variety of guidelines and hazard identification procedures to Esso Australia and other affiliated companies and provided advice and information. But it did not exercise any detailed oversight of Esso's activities. Its approach was ultimately laissez-faire, leaving responsibility for safety in Esso's hands. For instance, Exxon had not intervened to ensure that Esso identify the hazards associated with the interconnectedness of its Longford plants.

Perhaps the most dramatic example of Exxon's hands-off approach concerned the issue of cold metal embrittlement. Exxon itself recognised this as a hazard for its operations worldwide. In 1974 Exxon researchers published an article provocatively entitled "Will existing equipment fail by catastrophic brittle fracture?". Again, in 1983 researchers from the Exxon Research and Engineering Company published an article entitled "Brittle fracture of a pressure vessel: study results and recommendations". The article notes that:

brittle fractures of equipment sparked Exxon's recognition of the need for careful consideration of material toughness in the design and operation of pressure vessels and tankage for the past 25 years ...

Recognising that similar conditions could exist in other pressure vessels currently in service, a program was developed to establish a safe temperature for pressurisation of all Exxon equipment in refinery or chemical plant service ...

Equipment in the refineries fabricated prior to 1971 [Author's note – remember: gas plant 1 was built in 1969] *may not have the necessary toughness to resist brittle fracture at the lowest temperature of pressurisation.*

An Esso consultant described to the Commission a previous brittle fracture incident he had investigated:

[Certain events] *caused an exchanger to get super cold. They introduced a warm stream to it and it shuddered and just settled on the ground. It didn't explode and throw things all over the place, it just settled on the ground and caused a large vapour cloud.*

On this occasion the vapour cloud did not ignite, but this is the kind of incident about which Exxon was deeply concerned. As a result of this concern Exxon had inserted in its HAZOP guidelines the requirement that special attention be paid to the possibility of brittle fracture.

Somehow this concern had not been effectively transmitted to Esso Australia. Esso's general manager said he was not aware of the concern about brittle fracture expressed in the HAZOP guidelines. Moreover, Esso's most senior manager in charge of risk assessment was unaware of the two articles mentioned above and had not focused on the issue of brittle fracture. His explanation was that it was not his job. Unfortunately it was no one else's either. In further justifying his position he said: "nothing has been put in front of me that says, 'hey, you need to go out and chase catastrophic brittle fracture' ".

This is a critical comment. It suggests Esso Australia personnel can only be relied on to take action if *told* to. If so, this raises a serious question about Exxon's policy of advising and providing information, rather than instructing on crucial safety matters. If Esso Australia does not or cannot exercise responsibility effectively for the management of major hazards, perhaps that responsibility should be moved up the corporate hierarchy. The initial internal investigation of the Longford accident was carried out by a team from Exxon, not from Esso, on the grounds that they had the expertise which Esso lacked. If Exxon can take charge *after* the event, in this way, why not take charge *before* the event?

There is another reason why this makes sense in this case. Gas plant 1 was Esso's only plant susceptible to the loss of warm oil flow; the more recent gas plants 2 and 3 operated with very different technologies. Exxon, however, had 12 plants around the world using the same technology as gas plant 1. Its exposure to the risks of loss of warm oil flow were therefore far greater than Esso Australia's. Moreover, various Exxon plants around the world had suffered other cold brittle fractures, but judging by the evidence presented to the Commission, there had never been such an incident at Esso Australia plants. Exxon, in other words, had experience of cold brittle fracture; Esso had none. Exxon was in a position to learn from its own experience in this matter; Esso was not. Since Exxon had greater experience of and greater exposure to the problem, it seems eminently sensible for Exxon to take responsibility for it rather than leaving it to Esso.

The question of where in the corporate hierarchy responsibility for the management of major hazards should be located was also highlighted by the Moura disaster. Most coal mines have never had an explosion and most mine managers therefore have no direct reservoir of experience to draw on – no direct history to serve as a warning. The same was not true for the company which operates the Moura mine, BHP. This company had had two disastrous explosions in its mines in the preceding 15 years, one adjacent to Moura in 1986, which killed 12, and one at Appin, near Sydney in 1979 in which 14 miners died. BHP, in other words, had a history of explosions in its mines to learn from. Yet BHP left responsibility for preventing explosions in the hands of its mine managers. Clearly, this was a responsibility which should have been exercised further up the corporate hierarchy.

There is probably a general lesson here. The prevention of rare but catastrophic events should not be left to local managers with no experience of such events. Head office has both greater past experience and greater future exposure. Responsibility for prevention in these circumstances should be located at the top of the organisation. What this means in practice is the head office should maintain a team of experts whose job it is to spend time at all company sites ensuring that potentially catastrophic hazards have been properly identified. These people, of course, need the authority to insist that the necessary hazard identification procedures are implemented and they need to follow up to ensure that instructions have been carried out. Local managers must not be in a position to say: "no one told me to do it, so I didn't".

Before concluding this section it should be observed that Exxon and BHP are not alone in their policy of decentralising responsibility for safety. Many companies in this era of globalisation have restructured into horizontally-aligned independent units and this has often resulted in a drastic cutback in safety management from the centre. In ICI, for instance, the central safety, health and environment function virtually disappeared. According to one ICI official, "The central staff, which had grown from 20 to 72 during the 1980s contracted to just one employee by 1993" (quoted in Baram, 1998:199). The company subsequently recognised that it had gone too far and began reintroducing some central control. Likewise, the chief executive officer of BHP acknowledged in 1994 that the devolution of authority away from corporate headquarters had had a detrimental effect on safety (Prescott, 1994:6).

Conclusion

Managing major hazards requires that those hazards first be identified. In some industries, such as underground coal mining, the regulatory authorities in Australia have drawn up a list of major hazards which must be attended to. They then require that specific management plans be developed for each such hazard. In most industries, however, it is up to management to identify the major hazards and a great deal of time and effort may be necessary to do this effectively. It must also be understood that any significant change has the potential to introduce new hazards and the management of change must therefore include hazard identification processes. Esso understood this well, in principle, but in practice it failed to live up to these requirements.

Furthermore, it makes good sense for the head office of a company to take direct responsibility for the prevention of rare but catastrophic events. This is something which Exxon did not do. It is reasonable to conclude that Exxon's hands-off management strategy contributed to the Longford accident.

The previous chapter identified inadequate knowledge and training as a cause of the accident. This chapter pinpointed inadequate hazard identification as one reason for this inadequate knowledge. Furthermore, it was shown that this was in turn due to Esso's concern about costs and Exxon's inadequate oversight. But this is only the beginning of causal understanding: a series of other contributing factors will be identified in the following chapters.

Chapter

4

Ignoring Alarms:
Necessary Violations?

So far, not much has been said about the start of the accident sequence. It began with a strong flow of liquids from the offshore production platforms into the plant the evening before the accident. This led to a disturbance in normal operating conditions, not in itself an unusual event. But operators failed to control this upset and return the plant to normal, and the result of these continuing abnormal conditions was an automatic shutdown of the warm oil pumps next morning.

The question this raises is: why did the operators fail to control the process upset? As mentioned earlier, Esso's simplistic explanation was operator fault. One operator in particular had "ignored the alarms that he knew it was his job to react to, and the related process upset which he knew it was his job to attend to". This is hardly an enlightening response, but more than this, it is grossly unfair to the operator, as will shortly become apparent. A proper answer to the question will take us into the realm of the sociology of informal work practices and an examination of why it is that workers so often depart from the formal rules they are supposed to be following.

Meeting the gas order

The operators' job at Longford was to keep the process within specified limits of temperature, volume, flow and so on, despite variations in the quantity and quality of the input from Bass Strait and variations in output (sales) requirements. If the process went outside these limits, audible and visual alarms were triggered in the control room and theoretically the operators were supposed to bring the process back within the pre-determined limits. They were very conscious of the fact that variations in operating conditions might affect the quality of the gas produced, causing it to go "off spec", that is, to be no longer in accordance with the customer's specification. In short, they understood that process upsets had potential *commercial* consequences. But they were not aware that process upsets could affect the safety of the plant. It is important to bear this in mind in the following discussion of alarms.

For various reasons it was difficult for operators to maintain the process within the specified limits and the result was that there were frequent alarms. Ironically, it was easier at times to maintain the quality of the outgoing gas by allowing processing to occur outside the specified limits, that is, with some part of the system in alarm. Operators quickly cancelled the audible alarm but the visual alarm lights were less obtrusive and easier to live with. Here then is the beginning of a more complete explanation: the operators' understanding was that operating in alarm mode was sometimes necessary to meet the gas order for the day.

It is particularly important to note here that the condensate transfer system which had been installed in gas plant 1 in 1992 required the system to operate outside its normal temperature limits when condensate transfer was occurring. This disturbed the whole system and meant that certain other alarms occurred routinely and had to be tolerated (Dawson, 13.115).

One alarm, in particular, was frequently ignored. It concerned the level of condensate liquid in a certain vessel. This could be measured up to the so-called 100 per cent level. Higher levels were physically possible but were not measurable. The alarm was set at the 85 per cent level. Not only was the alarm routinely ignored, but the system was often operated for hours on end with levels so high that they were off scale, that is, above 100 per cent. Just how far above this level they went was unknown and unknowable with the existing equipment. One operator was asked at the inquiry:

You accept, though, that the control room operator's task was, so far as possible, to ensure that the level did not get above 100 per cent, or if it did, to bring it back below 100 per cent as soon as possible?

His answer was:

I would accept in theory that would be desirable but in practicality it's a very difficult thing to do with that particular control system.

The reason it was difficult is that the only effective way to deal with the problem was to reduce the flow of gas into the plant, which would have threatened production targets and made it more difficult to meet sales orders.

Unfortunately, operating the system in this condition had consequences the operators did not understand: condensate tended to overflow into other parts of the system. Following the stronger than usual flow of liquids into the plant the night before the accident, the system was operated above the 100 per cent level for many hours and it was the flow of excess condensate downstream that eventually caused the warm oil pumps to shut down.

The thinking of the operators is well captured in the following statement one of them made to the inquiry.

I don't think this has been properly brought out in the Commission, ... as operators [the production of gas] *is our job. Earlier you mentioned trouble shooting. That is not our foremost responsibility. Our first job is to provide gas on time, on spec at a given pressure. ... Everyone is asking questions about why we didn't take steps about high levels, but the prime concern to me, and I'm sure every other operator, is that we produce what we are supposed to, what we are paid to do.*

Despite this, counsel for Esso blamed one of the operators for allowing levels to go over 100 per cent. Even "a child [knows] ... how to stop the level of water increasing in his bath. He knows to either turn off the tap or pull the plug". As can now be appreciated, this comment seriously misrepresents the situation and is grossly unfair to the operators.

Alarm overload

The alarm problem was compounded enormously by the sheer number of alarms which operators were expected to deal with – at least three or four hundred a day! On one occasion an incident occurred which led Esso incident investigators to count the number of alarms. The figure for a 12-hour shift was 8,500 or 12 alarms every 60 seconds! The incident investigators apparently asked the operator at the time whether he felt comfortable dealing with so many alarms. His view was: "perhaps I didn't, but the fact remains that is what I'm paid to do". Given a situation of such extraordinary overload it was inevitable that operators would become desensitised and that alarms would not be properly attended to.

All alarms had to be responded to by silencing the audible alarm and switching the visual alarm from flashing mode to steady state. The visual alarm would then remain illuminated until the process had returned to normal. Many of these visual alarms were located on a computer screen which could only contain a certain number of alarm signals. Once that number was exceeded, existing alarms would be hidden by a new page of alarms and the earlier ones could only be accessed by scrolling backwards. Operators admitted, however, that it was not standard practice to scroll back to see which alarms were current. This meant they were often unaware of the status of many alarms. "To be aware of each and every one of them would be difficult, considering the volume of them", one of the operators told the inquiry.

This situation was exacerbated by the fact that if operators were not in the control room when alarms occurred, they might be acknowledged by passers-by, including maintenance workers, and no record was kept of who acknowledged such alarms. In these circumstances operators might be unaware that these alarms had occurred.

Many alarms were triggered by temporary fluctuations outside process limits and needed no remedial action. They were regarded as "nuisance alarms". Where an alarm was regarded as being nothing out of the ordinary it would be acknowledged without any attempt to investigate the reason.

Given the extraordinary situation of alarm overload, operators clearly needed to be highly selective in the alarms they attended to. There was no written guidance available from the company. So how did they decide? Here is what one operator said on the subject:

We become used to those that are requiring action straight away rather than those that may not necessarily require immediate action.

And how did they learn which is which?

By observation of how other operators treated that alarm, you pick up the correct measures to be taken in certain instances.

These are revealing statements. They suggest that operators have evolved amongst themselves a set of working rules to deal with the chaotic situation they faced. These rules enabled them to distinguish between alarms which needed attention, and those which could be tolerated or ignored, and enabled them, moreover, to respond to important alarms in a way which would allow them to continue meeting production targets. There is no reason to think that these were the optimal rules. Indeed they proved in the end not to be, since the failure of the operators to control the level of condensate allowed the accident sequence to develop. But until 25 September 1998, the rules had worked.

Counsel assisting the Commission described the situation in the following terms:

Over time a culture developed whereby it became normal to operate the plant in alarm. This culture developed despite the fact that the alarms existed for the primary purpose of alerting operators to that which was abnormal ... The consequence was that the protective purpose of the alarm system was lost ... The culture of operators regarding the operation of the plant in alarm was, in our submission, a contributing factor to the disaster.

What counsel didn't say, but should have, is that this culture was a natural and necessary adaptation to the otherwise impossible alarm overload situation which the operators faced.

The sociology of informal work practices

It is important to understand that Longford operators were not unusual in developing their own informal work procedures which differed from formal requirements. Sociological studies of work routinely reveal such patterns (eg Gouldner, 1954; Hynes & Prasad, 1997). In particular, analyses of disasters in complex technological environments routinely reveal that workers were not doing what the system designers intended them to do but were following procedures which they had improvised for themselves (Wynne, 1988:149). The interesting question, then, is why? In this section I shall describe some of the circumstances which give rise to these informal work procedures and consider the extent to which they illuminate what happened at Longford.

One situation in which informal rules evolve is when workers modify the system to achieve goals quite different from those originally intended by the system designers. These modifications may inadvertently undermine safety. Wynne (1988:155) provides an interesting example which came to light after a methane explosion which killed 16 people at an underground water supply valve house in the UK. The methane had accumulated in a large void in a water tunnel. The void was a result of an informal operator practice of leaving certain drainage valves a fraction open at all times to allow small quantities of silt to flush continually into a river. The officially required practice was to keep the valves fully closed usually, but to open them wide every few weeks to flush out the accumulated silt. But this practice muddied the clear river for days. Anglers had complained and operators had developed the continuous, slow flushing procedure to accommodate them. As Wynne notes, "no one had thought to warn them of the wider implications of this practice because they had evolved it themselves, unofficially ...".

But there is no parallel here with what happened at Longford. Esso's operators had developed informal rules to assist in achieving the *company's* goals, not for some cross-cutting purpose.

A second circumstance in which the informal rules diverge from the formal is when abnormality has been *normalised*. The classic example of this is the space shuttle, *Challenger*, which caught fire and plunged to earth in 1986 killing the seven astronauts on board (Vaughan, 1996). The integrity of the rockets depended on certain rubber seals known as O-rings. It had been discovered on several previous launches that they did not perform as required at low temperatures. Indeed, they malfunctioned. Nevertheless they had not failed totally. Over time, the malfunctioning was reconceptualised as normal and the risk of total failure came to be judged as acceptably low. The formal engineering expectation would be that if a critical component had not performed according to its design expectations, no further launches should occur until the component has been redesigned. What happened actually was that the design rules were progressively and informally changed to permit the degree of malfunction which had been shown by experience to be tolerable. The temperature on launch day was colder than at previous launches, but the technical malfunction had been normalised. The launch was thus given the go-ahead, and this time the seals failed totally, with catastrophic results.

Alarms are particularly susceptible to this process of normalisation. They are supposed to be warnings of abnormality, but if they occur in circumstances which are known to be normal, and hence tolerable, operators will quickly develop their own informal rules about how to deal with them, rules which diverge from what is formally expected. To bring this matter closer to home, many of us have worked in buildings where the tacit rule is that fire alarms are to be treated as false alarms and not as indicators of real danger, unless there is some independent confirmation of fire. If people did what they are theoretically supposed to do when alarms occur, work in many contexts would be seriously disrupted. Longford provides a clear example of this process. The conditions which generated alarms were frequently occurring and tolerable, and alarms were therefore normalised in the minds of workers.

There is an eerie similarity between the way alarms were dealt with at Longford and at Moura. At Moura, the mine atmosphere was automatically monitored for certain gases which would indicate that coal might be spontaneously burning in some remote part of the mine. This was a dire possibility, since burning coal could ignite any concentrations of methane which might be in the area. The results of mine gas monitoring were displayed on a computer terminal in an above-ground control room. In the days immediately prior to the explosion, the level of one indicator gas, which had been slowly rising, breached the alarm level on several occasions. Because the rate of increase had been slow, these alarms were cancelled without investigation. As at Longford, no record was kept of who acknowledged alarms and it was possible for unknown passers-by to do so. Moreover, alarms at Moura involved both a visual signal and an ear-splitting noise, and because they continued to occur intermittently, the set point or limit was raised so as to avoid the discomfort of what were regarded as nuisance alarms only. Had these alarms been responded to appropriately and the circumstances investigated closely, eleven lives would very likely have been saved. But circumstances had been normalised to such an extent that alarms had lost their function. The informal, experience-based rule had emerged – that alarms could be ignored with impunity.

A third and related situation in which tacit rules emerge is where workers encounter events unforeseen by the designer of the formal rules, which require that the rules be adjusted in order to get the job done. An important study by Bourrier (1998) shows how this was the situation confronting maintenance workers at a French nuclear power plant which she studied. She found that workers "performed small fixes without work orders, improvised new work sequences when they had overly generic procedures and left out parts of procedures they deemed inapplicable" (Bourrier 1998:137). They developed a great deal of "private knowledge" about actual work procedures and in the process became the experts; upper management had very limited knowledge of how problems were actually handled. Moreover, workers learned how to do their job during a long process of socialisation, a "compagnonnage" or apprenticeship, during which new workers learned from their more experienced counterparts just what the actual procedures were. The parallel with Longford operators is striking. They, too, had to modify the rules to keep production going and they, too, learned "the correct measures to be taken in certain instances" by observing other operators.

Various writers have suggested that this divergence of informal procedures from those formally laid down may well be inevitable. Reason (1999:73) speaks of "necessary violations" where non-compliance is "essential in order to get the job done". Similarly, Wynne (1988) claims that technology is essentially "unruly" in the sense that its rules of operation cannot be prescribed beforehand but emerge from practice: "technology involves making up rules and relationships as its practitioners go along". He draws an interesting inference from this, namely, that technology "is a form of social experiment on a grand scale" (Wynne 1988:158). He concludes that those who employ complex technologies should recognise that they can never guarantee to have these technologies under complete control and that therefore they can never guarantee safety. In short, as Bourrier comments, the idea that violations are necessary to get the job done has become almost a sociological law.

Formalising the informal

Bourrier's study of nuclear power stations was not confined to France; it was comparative, examining two nuclear power stations in the US as well. Her findings in 1992 were that the behaviour of maintenance workers in the US was dramatically different from their French counterparts and was in strict accordance with the formal rules. Given all the previous research, this is an unexpected and exciting result.

At Diablo Canyon power station the operating philosophy was "verbatim compliance". Operators had to comply with the letter of the law and the researcher found to her surprise that they did. Whenever they were confronted with an unexpected occurrence they called their supervisors rather than try to improvise. Likewise at the North Anna power station "each time they ran into an unplanned difficulty they would inform their foremen and seek their advice. They asked for a new work-order whenever the scope of the work was unclear" (Bourrier 1998:138).

What was it about the US power stations that facilitated this behaviour, apparently so contrary to the sociological norm? The answer is that at both US power stations the formal rules were flexible, in the sense that there were procedures by which they could be modified and updated quickly, procedures which also took careful account of the possible adverse consequences of change. The inevitable tendency for the formal and informal to diverge was dealt with, not by trying to bring informal practices into line with formal requirements – an impossible task – but by modifying the *formal* practices, in a sense to bring them into line with the *informal*.

At Diablo Canyon, modifying the rules was regarded as a full-time job and a group of engineers was specifically charged with this responsibility. There were as many engineers as foremen at the plant: 12 for the mechanical section, 8 for the electrical section, 10 for instrumentation and control, matching exactly the number of foremen in each section. In addition there were 20 procedure writers for the instrumentation and control section. During outages, that is, routine maintenance periods, the:

> *engineers leave their usual offices and go to the foremen's quarters ...* [where] *they are closer to the crews, ready to adjust, modify or rewrite any procedure with them. ... During outages section engineers have a chance to test, validate and improve their knowledge because they participate actively in problem solving ...* [S]*ection engineers are the final decision makers ...* [but] *both foremen and section engineers have to sign off on procedure updates. This requirement enhances cooperation and information exchange between the two groups.*

At North Anna, slightly different procedures achieve the same effect. These two power stations, then, provide evidence that routine rule violations are not inevitable in every organisation. Where the need for constant adjustments to operating procedures is acknowledged, organisations *can* prevent rule-violating procedures from developing – they can function as self-correcting organisations, as Bourrier calls them (1998:142).

It is obvious, however, that this is only possible where organisations are willing to commit abundant resources. This was the case in the nuclear power industry in the United States, following the near disaster in 1979 at the Three Mile Island nuclear power station. It was recognised that another such accident would mean the end of the entire industry and it was seen as imperative that this be avoided, no matter what the cost. As Rees (1994) has shown, this thinking led to a new approach to safety, drawn from the US nuclear navy's industrial principles. One of these principles, concerning technical self-sufficiency, read as follows:

> *Nuclear power is a technology whose complexity far exceeds that of other common methods of generating electricity ... It is essential that decision-making managers not only have extensive technical training themselves, but that they also have expert analytical and engineering resources readily available in their own organisation ...* (Rees, 1994:70).

The procedures which Bourrier has identified were clearly a response to this imperative.

Bourrier's findings are supported by studies of what are called high reliability organisations – nuclear aircraft carriers, air traffic control systems and so on (Weick, 1999). These are organisations where the potential for disaster is so great that failures are regarded as intolerable, to be avoided at any cost. Nuclear power stations in the US also began to function as high reliability organisations after the Three Mile Island accident (Rees, 1994). What these studies all show is that at critical times, extensive expert backup is available to operators to help with any difficulty. These experts are not just on call – they are there on the front line, observing what is happening and working with the operators. Air traffic control at major airports provides another good example. When traffic volume is low, a single controller does the job. As the traffic picks up, an associate controller assists. At high tempo "a third, often senior controller joins the two regulars as 'another pair of eyes'. At top tempo the area supervisor ... may also be nearby ..." (LaPorte & Consolini, 1991:38).

It is clear that high reliability depends on a degree of redundancy. High reliability organisations function with more people, and particularly more people with technical expertise, than are necessary to get the job done in the normal course of events. But when the course of events is not quite normal, when difficulties arise, this additional expertise swings into action. This is one of the features of these organisations which makes them so reliable – and safe.

The absence of engineering expertise at Longford

After this extensive detour into the sociology of informal work practices, it is now possible to apply these ideas to the case at hand. Esso was a company for which reliability was vital. The consequences of loss of production were potentially catastrophic, from a financial point of view. As it turns out, two weeks' interruption to the supply of gas has generated damages claims against Esso of more than one thousand million dollars. The implication of the preceding discussion is that in order to achieve high reliability, abundant engineering resources were needed to monitor and modify procedures to ensure that operators were not forced to improvise in ways that might ultimately prove to be disastrous. It is clear that, had engineering staff been working with operators on a daily basis, the practice of operating the plant in alarm for long periods could not have developed in the way it did. Engineers would have developed procedures to be followed in the event of alarms occurring and perhaps re-engineered the process to avoid the situation of massive alarm overload which the operators faced.

Until 1991, engineers had worked at Longford on a daily basis and had a detailed understanding of ongoing operations and constant interaction with plant operators. In 1992 Esso relocated all its plant engineers to Melbourne as part of a restructure designed to cut costs. It is significant that the condensate transfer system which exacerbated the problem of alarm overload came into operation in 1992, after the engineers had been withdrawn. The Commission commented on the withdrawal of engineers as follows:

> *The change appears to have had a lasting impact on operational practices at the Longford plant. The physical isolation of engineers from the plant deprived operations personnel of engineering expertise and knowledge which previously they gained through interaction and involvement with engineers on site. Moreover, the engineers themselves no longer gained an intimate knowledge of plant activities. The ability to telephone engineers if necessary, or to speak with them during site visits, did not provide the same opportunities for information exchange between the two groups, which are often the means of transfer of vital information* (Dawson, 13.81).

Not only would engineers on site have inhibited the development of a culture tolerant of alarms, but, according to one expert witness at the inquiry, the presence of engineers with a detailed familiarity with the plant would have led to a different outcome on the day of the accident. They would have recognised the significance of the leaks and the dangers of the very cold temperatures which were evident following the shutdown of the warm oil flow, and they would have recommended "that the plant was shut in, depressurised, thawed and that no hot liquid was introduced".

It is important to note that this witness was not asserting that *any* engineer would have come to this conclusion, but rather, one who had a detailed, day-to-day familiarity with plant operation. This could only be achieved by spending a long period "out on the plant following the shifts, basically crawling through the pipes getting a complete and full understanding of the operations, of the totality of that particular plant". This had been the training which one engineer described he had received at Longford in the late 1970s and he had subsequently functioned in much the same way as the engineers at Diablo Canyon, regularly assisting operators to deal with problems as they arose (Dawson, 13.131). This is this kind of engineering expertise which, according to the expert witness, would have averted the accident.

For the record, the Commission concluded that the transfer of engineers to Melbourne was "probably a contributing factor" to the accident (Dawson,15.7). Also for the record, Esso disagreed. It saw no connection between the accident and the relocation of the engineers. Esso's managing director explicitly rejected the need for on-site engineers, arguing at the Commission that "operations personnel are best placed, given their experience in operating plants, to deal with operating matters including process upsets". In the light of all the evidence to the contrary, this is a quite extraordinary claim. Another Esso director made the point that it was unusual to have engineers on-site at gas plants (Dawson, 2.69). In relying on industry practice in this way Esso had missed its chance to function as a high reliability organisation.

Surveillance from afar?

In transferring its engineers to Melbourne it was not Esso's intention to leave the Longford operators entirely to their own devices. Engineers were meant to carry out plant surveillance from a distance.

In principle this would have been possible by examining the continuously recorded data on temperature, condensate levels and so on. However, much of the information was recorded on charts which were not sent to Melbourne for analysis but simply thrown away (Dawson, 13.135). Perhaps because no use was being made of the data-recording charts, they were not maintained in good operating condition. On the day of the accident, 30 per cent of these recording systems were not working, either because they contained no paper or because the recording pens had run out of ink. It is clear that this situation had been allowed to develop because engineers in Melbourne were not in fact monitoring the plant from afar. According to counsel assisting the Commission:

The reality appears to be that nobody in Melbourne undertook any surveillance or monitoring role ... As a consequence, such information as may have been available to plant surveillance was not employed to assist operators to resolve process upsets, to identify unacceptable practices or to prevent the escalation of a process upset into a major hazard.

The Commissioners were highly critical of Esso for allowing this situation to exist. In their words:

The absence of regular monitoring of process operations by senior personnel in a high pressure hydrocarbon processing plant, which was not equipped with protective devices to make it completely fail-safe, exposed the plant to an unacceptable risk (Dawson, 13.137, emphasis added).

Conclusion

The accident sequence began because operators allowed the system to operate in alarm mode for many hours. Esso blamed the operators for this, claiming they ought to have known better. But operators claimed that they had to operate the system in this way to keep production going. There is nothing unusual about this. Studies of the behavior of workers routinely show that they are forced to develop informal, rule-violating practices in order to get the job done. These modifications are made with the best will in the world and work for long periods, enabling workers to get the job done. Unfortunately, however, these informal practices are all too often flawed in ways which lead eventually to disaster.

The question, then, is: can work systems be designed to overcome this ubiquitous problem? Studies of organisations for which high reliability is seen as vital suggest that the answer is yes. The trick is to be able to modify the formal rules with sufficient speed and flexibility that the need for informal modifications does not arise. However, the catch is that this requires a considerable commitment of resources, in particular, engineering resources.

In 1992 Esso turned its back on the possibility of high reliability operations at Longford by removing its engineers from site. In so doing it left the Longford operators to fend for themselves and they inevitably developed informal practices which in the end proved to be disastrous. It seems extraordinary that operators were allowed to operate the system in alarm for long periods, without any intervention by senior management. An Exxon investigator apparently told operators in the days following the explosion that on the day of the accident Longford was like a "runaway train" or a "rattlesnake ready to strike". These vivid images were intended to convey the idea that the plant was running out of control that day and that operators had no idea of what was about to happen. It is clear, though, that the imagery describes the situation which Esso had allowed to develop over a period of years; the company had lost control of the process long before the day of the accident.

Chapter

5

Communication:
Problems and Solutions

One of the recurrent findings in disaster research is that information that something was wrong was available somewhere within the organisation but was not communicated to relevant decision makers. Turner (1978) insists that all socio-technical disasters involve information or communication failures of this kind. They can be both horizontal – for example, the failure to transmit information between shifts, or vertical – the failure to pass bad news up the line to senior managers. The problem of vertical information flow has been noted by many writers. According to Stone (1975:89):

> in literally every case of corporate wrong-doing autopsied by myself and a group of University of Southern California law students, it turned out that someone down the corporate hierarchy was aware that trouble was brewing (usually for the company, in the last analysis, as well as for the public). For a variety of reasons the bad news never landed on the desk of someone who had both the authority and the inclination to do something about it.

The failure to pass information up the line is exemplified in the Challenger disaster. Information that earlier shuttle rockets had experienced technical problems was confined to one section of NASA and neutralised by a process of reinterpretation (see Chapter 4). Had this information been passed upwards to the highest ranking NASA officials a different set of decisions would have been made (Vaughan, 1996).

According to union safety official Yossi Berger (1999b:58), workers are often aware of information which might constitute a warning of danger but do not pass it on because they know it will not be well received. They do not even formulate it very clearly to themselves and it remains contained within what he calls the "mumbling environment", an environment of dark mutterings about management hypocrisy. In the next section I will provide some examples of these mutterings which, had they been picked up and responded to, would have led to a different outcome at Longford.

This chapter falls into two parts. The first examines aspects of the communication system at Longford and explores the reasons it failed to respond to the warnings that something might be amiss. Two major reporting systems will be examined: the routine reporting system and a specialised incident or near miss reporting system. The second part of the chapter will look at ways of overcoming these communication problems.

Routine reporting

A two-tier reporting system was in routine use at Longford. The bottom tier was constituted by the control room logs, filled in by operators at the end of every shift. The logs were supposed to contain information about process upsets, significant alarms and the like (Dawson, 13.96). In practice, very little of this information found its way into the log books, which were filled out in a very casual manner. However, for all their defects, the logs did contain numerous entries which would have alerted a careful reader to the existence of problems. Consider, for example: "TRC3A is very cold, could not find a reason why, or how to warm it up", or "flaring LPG accumulators due to hundreds of upsets". These were clear and quite specific indicators that all was not well. Even more dramatic were the following: "mayhem" and "place is stuffed". Here, captured in the log books entries, is Berger's "mumbling environment". Here are the warnings that the process was essentially out of control. Unfortunately, management did not read these reports (Dawson, 13.108).

Management's failure to read operator logs might not have mattered if the warnings they contained had found their way into the second reporting tier – the shift supervisors' reports. But these were filled out without reference to the control room logs and did not contain references to safety-related matters. Supervisors' reports were maintained on computers and were widely available, but by this stage the warnings had already been filtered out and effectively lost.

The result was that the manager of the Longford plant confessed to being unaware of a number of warning signs which had occurred in the months prior to the accident. In practice he relied on oral communication rather than written reports. He explained at the Commission that he would expect to be told about any significant incident at morning meetings. It is clear, however that this reliance on oral communication was misplaced. According to his own evidence, he was not told about important matters recorded in the operator logs.

There is a remarkable similarity here with the reporting system which operated at Moura mine. It was also a two-tier system. The bottom level contained safety-relevant information and indeed critical warnings that the mine was in danger, while the second level, filled out by the shift supervisor, contained information about production during the shift and systematically omitted safety considerations. Just as at Longford, neither shift supervisors nor their superiors regularly read the first tier reports and the result was that critical warning signs were missed. Just as at Longford, managers expected to be told orally about any matters of significance, and just as at Longford, they frequently weren't.

The fact that both sites operated a two-tier routine reporting system with safety-relevant information confined to the lower tier raises the intriguing question of how widespread this particular phenomenon might be. It is a question that cannot be answered here. What is undoubtedly widespread is the failure of management to read routine shift reports. Such reports contain much that is not of relevance for more senior managers and it is to be expected that they will not read them. But nor can it be assumed that any critical information contained in these reports will be drawn to their attention, orally. There is much evidence that it won't. What is needed is a more systematic procedure for flagging important matters and passing them up the line. Such a system will be outlined later in this chapter.

Communication between shifts

It is widely recognised that safety and efficiency in round-the-clock operation depends on good communication between shifts. For this reason Esso required its operators and shift supervisors to have face-to-face contact at shift hand-over. The operators' logs were intended to facilitate communication between shifts about problems currently being experienced.

Unfortunately, this communication was less than adequate. Consider the communication at the beginning of the shift on which the accident occurred. The operator log for the previous shift made no mention of the off-scale condensate levels which, as described in Chapter 4, were a precursor to the accident. Nor did it mention other associated problems which the operator had experienced or the many alarms which had occurred. This might not have mattered if this information had been conveyed in face-to-face communication at shift hand-over. But it wasn't, no doubt because, as previously described, these adverse conditions were so normal that the operator did not think to mention them. The result was that the incoming operator did not know about the alarms in relation to the high level of condensate. The Commission concluded that had the incoming operator's attention been drawn to these matters he might have managed the situation differently and prevented the accident sequence from developing (Dawson, 13.103).

This point is worth developing. The level of condensate was in part controlled by a hand-operated valve known as the TRC3B by-pass valve. Closing the valve increased the efficiency of the process and enhanced the value of the output from the plant (Dawson, 3.19), but it also meant that the level of condensate would rise (2.10-11) above its set level, with increased risk of spillover into other parts of the system. The valve had to be adjusted frequently to balance these competing requirements.

Because of the inadequate communications between shifts, operators and their supervisors were unaware of how their counterparts on previous shifts had been dealing with the problem and each new shift seemed to adjust the valve without reference to the conditions of the previous shift which had led to the current valve position. So dramatic was this situation that one operator described it as a "tug of war between two supervisors" on different shifts. One wanted it open and the other, closed.

At the beginning of the fatal shift, the on-coming operator, unaware of the high condensate levels experienced on the previous shift, closed the valve, which would have had the effect of raising the condensate level even higher (Dawson, 3.25-6). This action was critical in allowing the accident sequence to develop. In short, communication failure at shift hand-over was one of the many causes of this accident – cause in the sense that, but for this communication failure, the accident would probably not have occurred (Dawson, 13.103).

Esso's incident-reporting system

In addition to its routine reporting system Esso maintained a reporting system for non-routine incidents. An incident was explained in Esso's Safety Management Manual as an unplanned event that caused or *could have* caused injury or damage to personnel, property or the environment. Esso required all incidents, no matter how minor, to be reported to a supervisor and recorded on a hard copy incident form. Near misses, which could have resulted in injury or damage in slightly different circumstances, are incidents according to the explanation above and are therefore included in the reporting requirement.

An incident report was the key trigger for a thorough-going incident investigation. If the reported incident was regarded as serious or potentially serious it was subjected to a root cause analysis to identify all the factors which may have contributed to it.

The definition of incident is wide enough to encompass serious process upsets such as leaks and unexpectedly cold temperatures. But such matters almost never found their way into the incident reporting system and therefore failed to trigger any incident investigation. Even process upsets serious enough to lead to temporary shutdown of the plant failed to enter the reporting system. Nor were any of the process upsets, which operators recorded in the control room logs, reported in this way. Had they been, the many warnings contained in the logs might have received the attention they deserved. There was no good reason for these omissions. Management's view was that it was up to the operators to report matters if they thought they had an "escalation potential". But in practice, neither operators nor staff seemed to have considered the escalation potential of process upsets.

A dramatic example of this failure was the cold temperature incident which occurred on 28 August, just a month before the accident. This incident was in some respects a preview of what happened on 25 September. One of the warm oil pumps developed a leak which had to be repaired. The backup pump was out of action, and this meant that the warm oil system had to be closed down to carry out the work. The system had probably never been closed down in this way before and there were no written procedures to follow. As a precaution, the flow of gas into the plant was cut right back. Nevertheless, following the cessation of warm oil flow the heat exchangers became super cold. As a result, a coating of ice appeared on pipe work which was normally too hot to touch, and one of the heat exchangers sprang a substantial leak. This is exactly what happened a month later, except that the shutdown of the warm oil system on 25 September was unplanned and caused by process upsets elsewhere in the system. The August incident did not end in disaster, more by good luck than design, for none of those concerned recognised the dangers of the situation.

The super cold temperatures which were evident during the August shutdown constituted a serious incident which Esso later said should have been reported. No one had ever seen ice on these pipes before. Had the matter been reported it would have triggered an incident investigation which would have identified the possibility of cold temperature embrittlement of the heat exchangers and the dangers of brittle fracture (Dawson, 13.148). In short, had the incident been reported it would have been recognised as the clear warning of danger it was. Here, then, is a particularly dramatic illustration of the point with which this chapter began, namely, that every disaster is preceded by warning events which, if recognised as such, would have enabled the disaster to be averted.

There was one major exception to the general failure to report process upsets. Where such an upset impacted on customers, it was treated as a reportable incident. This might be the case if the quality of the gas supplied to the customer went "off spec" or if the quantity of gas required could not be supplied. These matters triggered significant follow-up investigations. There is a certain irony here. Process upsets which may have had minor commercial consequences, were dealt with thoroughly; those which had the potential for devastating commercial consequences were not.

If the incident reporting system was not used, on the whole, to report serious process upsets, what *was* it used for? Its primary use was to report incidents which caused, or had the potential to cause, routine lost-time injuries to individuals – "slips trips and falls", as they were referred to at various points in the proceedings. Workers, were somewhat resistant to the idea that they should have to fill out forms every time they cut a finger or fell off a bicycle, as they put it. Esso, however, put considerable energy into trying to get workers to report such matters and repeatedly urged them at tool box meetings to do so. Why the incident reporting system was used in this way is an important question to be addressed in the next chapter. Suffice it to say, at this point, that using it as a tool for dealing with lost-time injuries undermined its value for disaster prevention.

Designing a reporting system to avert disaster

It has already been noted that prior to any disaster there will nearly always be information somewhere within the organisation that trouble is brewing. This certainly applied to Esso at Longford. Critical information must not be allowed to lie around unrecognised, ignored, or buried like some landmine waiting to be triggered. The challenge is to find ways to assemble this information and move it up the hierarchy to the point where it can be understood and acted on responsibly. In this section, I want to suggest a way this might be done which avoids some of the pitfalls described above.

Any company which faces major hazards is likely to have an e-mail system or something similar which can greatly facilitate the flow of information up the hierarchy. The suggestions which follow depend largely on this kind of technology.

Triggers

The starting point is an incident or near miss reporting system. But if this is to have any chance of gathering relevant warning signs, management must put considerable thought into specifying what sorts of things should be reported: what are the warning signs at this workplace that something might be about to go disastrously wrong? Once identified, these signs must be treated as triggers to action, and management must specify what kind of action is required and who is responsible for taking the action. For instance: should a further investigation be undertaken? Should production be stopped? The requirement to identify trigger events is now built into guidelines for controlling major hazards in the mining industry in Queensland and New South Wales.

Here are some examples of the kinds of events which management might decide need to be treated as warning signs:

- certain kinds of leaks;

- certain kinds of alarms;

- particular temperature, pressure or other readings;

- certain maintenance problems; and

- machinery in a dangerous condition.

Routine reports

Management should also consider whether anyone on site is required to fill out an end-of-shift report. If so, might these reports contain warning information which should be entered into the reporting system? They certainly did at Longford and at Moura. Management will need to specify what kinds of items in routine reports should be entered into the system. Being selective in this way will serve to flag information in these reports that needs attention and avoid the problem of information overload inherent in routine reporting.

Worker initiatives

Workers on site should be encouraged to report not only matters which management has specified but also any other matters about which they are concerned. In some circumstances they will be reluctant to make reports for fear of reprisals. Management will need to find ways to overcome this fear.

Once workers begin to take reporting initiatives, experience suggests the reports are likely to be about things in need of maintenance or fixing. Management will need to carry out the suggested work, whether or not it seems necessary from an accident prevention point of view, so as to demonstrate good faith. Workers at Longford complained that the company was unwilling to carry out maintenance work which they requested, thus undermining their incentive to report. It is perhaps symptomatic of the failure of Esso's reporting system that the company's managing director was able to tell the Commission he had no knowledge of the frustration which operators were experiencing in getting maintenance work done. As I shall show in the next chapter the maintenance backlog was one of the factors which contributed to the explosion.

Feedback

It is not enough that people make reports or pass information up the line. The outcome must be fed back in the form of a written response to the person who made the initial report. This will improve the morale of reporters and they will be motivated to take the reporting process more seriously. In the absence of such feedback, reporting systems are likely to break down. Workers at Esso who made incident reports did not necessarily get any feedback from management about their reports and this no doubt contributed to their reluctance to report.

Feedback is important, not only to ensure that reporters take the process seriously, but also to obligate those to whom they report to act on reports conscientiously. Many companies now have reporting systems which specify action to be taken and the person responsible for taking the action. The best companies attempt to "close the loop" by requiring the person who is responsible for taking an action to sign off when he or she has taken it. But even this may not be enough to ensure that the action taken is effective. The principle of feedback requires that the person who initially raised the concern be notified of what action has been taken.

Feedforward

To be truly effective the process must not terminate at this point. The next step is to require the person who initially raised the matter to indicate whether the action taken is satisfactory in his or her view. Where the initiator is not satisfied the matter should cycle through the system again until such time as the initiator is satisfied, or alternatively, some senior manager of the company is prepared to over-ride the concerns of the initiator, in writing. There is evidence that in the right circumstances workers are indeed willing to indicate if they think an initial response is unsatisfactory and to pursue the matter at a higher level (ACIL, 1998:13).

Escalation

Reporting systems must specify a time by which management must respond, and people making reports should be able to some extent to specify how urgent the matter is and therefore how quickly they require a response, eg within a day, within a week, within a month. The initial response may of course be to explain that more time is needed to deal with the matter.

If the person to whom the report is made does not respond within the required time the system must escalate, that is, send the message further up the corporate hierarchy. This not only draws the attention of more senior managers to the problem but also alerts them to the fact that their subordinates may not be responding appropriately. This chain of escalation should end up on the screen of the CEO.

CEO response

Whether this whole system works depends, ultimately, on whether the person at the top of the information chain, the CEO, is committed to making it work. If the CEO allows messages to sit unanswered on his or her screen the system may end up a flop. But if the CEO responds by asking why messages have not been answered further down the line, the chances are the system will work. At one mine site I have visited where such a system is being implemented, when the escalation process was "switched on" about 30 messages went through to the general manager. Some of these were caused by supervisors going on leave and not designating people to deal with their messages and some were the result of supervisors simply failing to respond to messages. The general manager expressed considerable annoyance that messages had escalated all the way to his desk and thereafter the system began to work well.

Auditing

Such systems must be carefully audited, that is, tested to see if they are capturing the intended information. One such test is to track some of the information flows which have occurred to see whether bad news, or at least news of problems, is being entered into the system and responded to. This may mean, for example, sifting through end-of-shift reports to see whether relevant items have indeed made it into the reporting system. This kind of auditing at Esso would have revealed numerous items which should have been entered into the incident reporting system but weren't. Another audit strategy might be to enter a test warning into the reporting system and see how the system responds. Experience shows that no reliance should be placed on the system described above unless and until it passes these kinds of tests. (For further discussion see Hopkins, 1999:29-36.)

Anonymity, confidentiality and immunity from discipline

A feature of the kinds of warning signs which I have described above is that they do not involve any obvious fault or mistake on the part of any one person and certainly not on the part of the reporter. They are impersonal indicators of danger. However, where incidents reflect badly on the reporter or on some other individual who might be in a position to retaliate against the reporter, there are obvious disincentives to reporting. If the system depends on this kind of information it must be designed to overcome these disincentives. In particular, the following issues must be resolved:

- should anonymous reports be accepted?
- how can confidentiality be guaranteed?
- should reporters be provided with any immunity from discipline?

There are no simple answers to these questions and organisations answer them in different ways, depending on their particular circumstances. One context in which these issues have been extensively dealt with is the aviation industry, which has developed a variety of incident reporting schemes. These may be models for other industries in some circumstances. Perhaps because the potential for disaster in the field of aviation is so great, most of these schemes have been introduced on an industry-wide basis, by government agencies. Many countries, including Australia, operate mandatory reporting schemes, that is schemes which require by law the reporting of accidents and specified incidents such as near mid-air collisions. Reporters are necessarily identified and the level of reporting in such schemes turns out to be very sensitive to the degree of immunity granted to reporters. In 1968, when the US Federal Aviation Authority gave immunity from prosecution to pilots who reported near collisions, the reporting rate trebled. When immunity was removed three years later the reporting rate dropped to below its pre-1968 level (Pidgeon, 1997:10).

In addition to mandatory systems, various countries, including Australia, operate a voluntary and confidential aviation incident reporting scheme, where people are encouraged to report not just specified incidents but anything of concern. Anonymous reports are not accepted because, in the words of the Australian agency which receives the reports, "they do not allow us to establish how serious the reporter is or to investigate the report in sufficient detail to have something to pass on to a suitable authority" (BASI, 1995:27). Reporters therefore must provide their names to the agency, but, in order to ensure confidentiality, after the report has been verified and further details obtained, identifying information is removed and the source is no longer traceable. This means that reporters are protected from any possibility of disciplinary action or retaliation. But as a consequence, reporters cannot be provided with direct feedback about action taken, nor given an opportunity to comment on the adequacy of the response. This scheme has generated an enormous amount of useful information, for example, about problems seeing other aircraft at night on taxiways, temporary cranes erected dangerously close to runways and so on. Such information could hardly be specified beforehand for the purposes of mandatory reporting but clearly provides an early warning of problems.

The confidential nature of these voluntary schemes is seen as vital to their success in the aviation industry. However, in contexts where confidentiality is not such an issue, as described in the previous section, success is likely to depend on the opposite approach, namely the identification of reporters, so they can be provided with feedback and the opportunity to comment on the response, thus maximising their incentive to report.

Industry-wide schemes are probably only viable where there is an active industry regulatory body. But reporting schemes also operate internally in many companies. Within companies there is an additional mechanism which can be put in place to encourage the reporting of near misses and incidents which don't result in injury. If the number of near misses reported is regarded as a positive indicator and included in some way in managers' performance appraisals, then managers themselves will find ways to encourage their subordinates to report (ACIL, 1998:20).

One other scheme, operated by British Airways, will be mentioned here because of its wider potential. On every flight a large number of parameters are continuously recorded using flight data recorders ("black boxes"). This information is downloaded and computer searched for instances where these parameters have exceeded safe limits; for instance, excessive rates of ascent or descent, or hard landings. When such cases are identified, the pilots are contacted for a full account of the incident. The system is one which maintains the confidentiality of the pilots and reports, which do not disclose the name of the reporter, go to management for the purposes of organisational learning (Pidgeon, 1997:9). In a sense, what this process does is identify situations where incident reports might have been expected and then request the missing reports.

This model can be generalised. In any industrial activity where processes are continuously monitored and recorded, the data can, in principle, be searched for instances of abnormality. When such instances are found, operators can be asked for more information about the circumstances. Such an approach would seem to be readily applicable to industries like gas processing. At Longford, such data was indeed recorded but there was no system for searching the data for anomalous situations.

Conclusion

Communication failures are implicated in every disaster. There is always information somewhere in the system which, if responded to appropriately, would have averted the disaster. According to Turner (1978:195) the central question to ask, then, is: "What stops people from acquiring and using appropriate advance warning information so that large-scale accidents and disasters are prevented?". In Esso's case the answer is that the incident reporting system was not being used to report process upsets. Instead, for reasons to be addressed in the next chapter, it was used as a tool for reporting and preventing relatively minor injuries. Moreover, there was no mechanism for highlighting safety-relevant information in operators' end-of-shift reports. This meant that communication between shifts about crucial matters was less than adequate and, furthermore, that important warning information contained in these logs was not transmitted up the line.

Companies operating in high-risk industries need to put considerable thought into designing incident reporting systems which will capture relevant warning signs. This involves specifying as far as possible the kinds of things which will count as warnings and requiring that they be reported. Wherever possible, feedback mechanisms must be built in, both to encourage reporters and to increase the likelihood that something effective will be done about reports. Where the relevant warning information is potentially detrimental to the reporter, confidentiality requirements may make effective feedback impossible. Companies may need to design systems which allow for both types of reporting.

Chapter

6

Esso's Approach to Safety

A critical question was left hanging in the last chapter: why did Esso use the incident-reporting system as a tool for reducing the number of lost-time injuries, rather than to provide warnings which might help it avoid catastrophic accidents? To answer this question we need to understand Esso's approach to safety.

Esso's safety record

Esso regarded itself as a safety conscious company. Following standard industry practice, it used lost-time injury frequency rate as its principal measure of safety performance, and in terms of this measure Esso's level of safety was enviable. The previous year, 1997, had passed without a single lost-time (LTI) injury and Esso Australia had won an industry award for this performance. It had completed thirteen million work hours without a lost-time injury to an Esso employee and assisted its contractor workforce to achieve more than 3 million work hours free of lost-time injury (Smith, 1997:15). Moreover, Esso's performance had been sustained; its LTI statistics for the whole period from 1990 to 1998 had been well ahead of the industry average.

Reporting the number of hours worked without lost-time injury puts enormous pressure on workers not to spoil the tally by reporting an injury, and the greater the number of hours free of injury the greater the pressure not to report. Moreover, it has been observed in another context that companies which achieve extraordinary LTI results often do so by carefully managing the measure, as well as managing safety

(Hopkins, 1999:89). In particular, companies which are assessed on the basis of their LTI performance, may resort to bringing the "walking wounded" back to work on alternate duties, the day after an accident, to prevent the accident counting as a lost-time injury (Hopkins, 1995). This has presumably occurred at Esso, on occasion.

Of course, there are good reasons to get injured workers back on the job as quickly as possible, and effective and legitimate claims/injury management may convert what are potentially lost-time injuries into injuries without lost time. But it is clear that this injury/claims management process means that the recorded LTI rate is a thoroughly misleading indicator of the extent of injury.

Esso itself provides the following illustration of the inadequacy of LTI figures as a measure of injury rates. In 1993 it achieved five million hours worked by its own employees (not contractors) without a single lost-time injury. At the same time the company's health and safety newsletter carried the following report.

While the five million workhour LTI free achievement ... has been pleasing, there is concern about the number of fall-related incidents and injuries. The most serious incident occurred when a casual platform assistant/primary first aider suffered a serious injury from a fall down the stairs from the helideck on Halibut platform. He suffered bruising, ligament damage and concussion and was medivaced via helicopter and ambulance to Gippsland Base Hospital in Sale (13/9/93).

The newsletter goes on to report other, "relatively serious" injuries to employees. None appears to have resulted in any lost time. Even the man transported ashore by medivac was apparently back at work for his next shift, possibly on alternate duties at some Esso facility on shore.

To overcome this problem Esso keeps data on total recordable injuries, defined as injuries which require medical treatment, or which prevent the injured person from performing any part of their normal duties. In May 1998, just four months before the Longford accident, the company had gone six months without a single recordable injury.

It is possible to be sceptical about these figures, as well. Workers employed by an Esso subcontractor know that their employer may be called upon by Esso to account for an incident which has been reported. With the casualisation of employment there is no guarantee of continuing work, and workers are sometimes fearful that if they have embarrassed the subcontractor in this way, they may find their services no longer required. To avoid this outcome, they may request first aid on an unofficial or unrecorded basis or forgo it altogether.

It should be reiterated that none of this discussion is intended to imply that Esso is unconcerned about safety. It is interesting to note that one of the operators whom Esso later blamed for the accident spoke up for the company during an interchange at the inquiry:

Does that indicate to you that the primary role and the primary concern (of Esso) is supply (of gas)?—

That, in my view, would be unfair on the company

Yes?—

Because the company has a strong emphasis on safety

Yes?—

The questions you've asked me this morning have been such that it indicates that our main emphasis is supply, and I've in some terms, agreed with you, but I want to stress that the company has always been big on safety.

Measuring safety in hazardous industries

Quite apart from the issues of under-reporting discussed above, measuring safety in terms of lost-time injuries or total recordable injuries is inherently problematic in hazardous industries. To understand why, we need to make a distinction between, on the one hand, high frequency/low severity events such as slips, trips and falls, which result in injury to single individuals and, on the other hand, low frequency/high severity incidents such as explosions and major fires, which may result in multiple fatalities. LTI data are largely a measure of the number of routine industrial injuries; explosions and major fires, precisely because they are rare, do not contribute to the LTI figures in the normal course of events. LTI data are thus, at best, a measure of how well a company is managing minor hazards; they tell us nothing about how well major hazards are being managed. Moreover, firms normally attend to what is being measured, at the expense of what is not. Thus a focus on LTIs can lead companies to become complacent about their management of major hazards. This is exactly what seems to have happened at Esso.

Precisely the same phenomenon contributed to the explosion at Moura. By concentrating on high frequency/low severity problems Moura had managed to halve its lost-time injury frequency rate in the four years preceding the explosion, from 153 injuries per million hours worked in 1989/90 to 71 in 1993/94. By this criterion, Moura was safer than many other Australian coal mines. But as a consequence of focusing on relatively minor matters, the need for vigilance in relation to catastrophic events was overlooked.

Clearly, the lost-time injury rate is the wrong measure of safety in any industry which faces major hazards. An airline would not make the mistake of measuring air safety by looking at the number of routine injuries occurring to its staff. Baggage handling is a major source of injury for airline staff, but the number of injuries experienced by baggage handlers tells us nothing about flight safety. Moreover, the incident and near miss reporting systems operated in the industry are concerned with incidents which have the potential for multiple fatalities, not lost-time injuries.

The challenge then is to devise new ways of measuring safety in industries which face major hazards, ways which are quite independent of lost-time injuries. Positive performance indicators (PPIs) are sometimes advocated as a solution to this problem. Examples of PPIs include the number of audits completed on schedule, the number of safety meetings held, the number of safety addresses given by senior staff and so on. The main problem with such indicators is that they are extremely crude measures and are unlikely to give any real indication of how well major hazards are being managed. It is not the number of audits which have been conducted but the quality of audits which is crucial for major hazard management. Unfortunately, the quality of audits is not something which is easily measured. PPIs are said to have the advantage of getting away from the indicators of failure, such a LTIs or total recordable injuries. As I shall demonstrate below, however, there is nothing inherently wrong with indicators of failure.

Perhaps because the prevention of major accidents is so absolutely critical for nuclear power stations, it is this industry, at least in the

United States, which has taken the lead in developing indicators of plant safety which have nothing to do with injury or fatality rates. Since nuclear power generation provides a model in some respects for petro-chemical and other process industries, let us consider this case a little further. The indicators include: number of unplanned reactor shutdowns (automatic, precautionary or emergency shutdowns), number of times certain other safety systems have been automatically activated, number of significant events (carefully defined) and number of forced outages (see Rees, 1994:chap 6). There is wide agreement in the industry that these are valid indicators, in the sense that they really do measure how well safety is being managed.

Certain features of these indicators are worthy of comment. First, they are negative indicators, in the sense that the fewer, the better. The proponents of positive performance indicators argue that where failures are rare (eg nuclear reactor disasters) it is necessary to get away from measures of failure and adopt "positive" measures of the amount of the effort being put into safety management. What lies behind this argument is the fact that where failures are rare it is not possible to compute failure rates which will enable comparisons between sites to be made or trends over time at one site to be identified. Such information is necessary if the effectiveness of management activity is to be assessed. But the failures mentioned above (reactor shutdowns and the like) *are* common enough in nuclear power stations to be useful for these purposes. The point is that measures of failure are fine as long as the frequency of failures is sufficient to enable us to talk of rates.

Second, these indicators are "hard", in the sense that it is relatively clear what is being counted. A shutdown is a shutdown. This is not true of positive indictors such as number of audits. Audits are of varying quality, from external, high-powered investigations to the internal, tick-a-box exercises. If companies are assessed on number of audits, they may respond with large numbers of low quality audits.

Third, the indicators described above are industry-specific. Whereas LTI rates have the advantage that they can be used to compare safety in different industries, indicators such as the number of reactor shutdowns cannot be used in this way. But being industry-specific means that they *are* common to all nuclear power stations and *can* therefore be used to make comparisons between power stations. This is their particular strength. The industry body collects the figures and regularly presents them to meetings of nuclear industry CEOs. This generates a highly competitive response and poor performers are shamed into doing better. The result has been a steady improvement in safety, as measured by these indicators.

The model works in the nuclear industry because the industry body is powerful enough to mandate the collection of relevant data and to prevent under-reporting. Whether it can work in other hazardous industries probably depends on the strength of their industry associations and the depth of concern in the industry to avoid disaster. If it is to work, what is required is careful consideration and industry agreement on the kinds of failures to be counted. Moreover, there must be enough players in the field to make comparisons possible. This would require a national or even international arena of contest. Finally, regular meetings of CEOs would need to occur so that the shaming potential of the process could be realised (Braithwaite, 1989).

There is an obvious opportunity for confusion between the performance indicators discussed above and the incident and near miss reporting systems described in Chapter 5. An incident and near miss reporting system is designed to capture warnings of trouble and pass them up the line to responsible decision-makers. In some sense the indicators of failure mentioned in this chapter are also warnings of trouble. But they are warnings that are sufficiently clearly defined and unmistakable so that reporting can be mandated on an industry-wide basis and not easily evaded. They would therefore constitute only a very small subset of matters which could potentially be reported in an incident and near miss reporting system.

The culture of safety

Let us return to Esso's case to consider in more detail how its approach to safety was distorted by its focus on LTIs. The key to its approach was the creation of a *safety culture*. Prior to the accident, the company's safety adviser argued that:

> *safety performance has been achieved through an unwavering commitment and dedication from all levels in the organisation to*

create a safety culture which is genuinely accepted by employees and contractors as one of their primary core personal values (Smith, 1997).

The aim is to "create a *mindset* that no level of injury (not even first aid) is acceptable" (emphasis added). Esso's safety theme, "Let's get real ... all injuries are preventable", was explicitly aimed at achieving this mindset (Smith, 1997:16).

Esso draws an interesting implication from this. Since safety is about a mindset, it is something which the individual must cultivate 24 hours a day. It cannot be exclusively about occupational safety but must include safety in the home. Hence Esso's 24-hour safety program. This is how Esso's safety adviser expresses it:

Real commitment to safety can't be "turned on" at the entrance gate at the start of the day and left behind at the gate on the way home. Safety and well-being of fellow employees is extended beyond the workplace at Esso. A true commitment to safe behaviour is developed by promoting safety as a full-time (i.e. 24-hour) effort both on and off the job (Smith, 1997:22).

A number of features of this conception of safety culture deserve comment. First, it sees a culture as a matter of *individual* attitudes – attitudes which can be cultivated at work, but which in the final analysis are characteristics of individuals, not the organisations to which they belong. This view of culture is widespread in the business world (see the trenchant critique by Berger, 1999b:57). It contrasts with the sociological and anthropological view of culture as a characteristic of a group and not something which the individual can take from one context to another, from home to work, for example.

Second, in Esso's view culture is about *attitudes* and *values*. An alternative conception is that culture is about *practices*. Note that practices are characteristics of groups or organisations. They are essentially *collective* practices. Reason argues, quoting an organisational anthropologist, that this is a more useful concept when thinking about safety culture.

Changing collective values of adult people in an intended direction is extremely difficult, if not impossible. Values do change, but not according to someone's master plan. Collective practices, however, depend on organisational characteristics like structures and systems, and can be influenced in more or less predictable ways by changing these (Hofstede, quoted in Reason 1997:194).

Reason suggests that the practices which make up a safety culture include such things as effective reporting systems, flexible patterns of authority and strategies for organisational learning. These are clearly organisational, not individual, characteristics.

Third, in Esso's conception of a safety culture, the role of management is to encourage the right mindset among the workers. It is the attitudes of workers which are to be changed, not the attitudes of senior management.

Fourth, a presumption which underlies Esso's approach is that accidents are within the power of workers to prevent and that all that is required is that they develop the right mindset and exercise more care in the way they do their work. We are back here to the human error explanation of accidents. Esso's safety adviser is quite explicit about this: "human error can account for 70 per cent to more than 80 per cent of incidents" (Smith, 1997:25).

It is clear therefore that Esso's safety culture approach, *in principle*, ignores the latent conditions which underlie every workplace accident (see Chapter 2) and focuses instead on the workers' attitudes as the cause of the accident. Take the case, mentioned above, of the man who fell down the stairs from the helideck. The idea of safety culture as mindset attributes this accident to worker carelessness and ignores the possible contribution of staircase design to the accident. Despite this drawback, Esso's approach *is* potentially relevant to minor accidents – slips, trips and falls – which individuals *may* possibly avoid simply by exercising greater care. Esso is quite clear that this is its purpose. All its recent initiatives such as the 24-hour safety program and its stepback five by five program (see Chapter 3), were motivated by the fact that its rate of minor injuries had stopped declining and new strategies were needed to reduce the rate further. Moreover, according to Smith, the new initiatives have been successful in this respect.

But creating the right mindset is not a strategy which can be effective in dealing with hazards about which workers have no knowledge and which can only be identified and controlled by management. Many major hazards fall into this category. The risk of cold metal embrittlement is a case in point. As has been described, workers had no understanding that this was a risk facing the plant on the day of the accident and had no awareness of the danger they were in. It follows that no mindset or commitment to safety on their part would have led to a different outcome. As described in Chapter 3, it was up to management to identify and control the hazards concerned and management had not done this adequately.

There is an interesting implication here. If culture, understood as mindset, is to be the key to preventing major accidents, it is management culture rather the culture of the workforce in general which is most relevant. What is required is a *management* mindset that every major hazard will be identified and controlled and a *management* commitment to make available whatever resources are necessary to ensure that the workplace is safe. The Royal Commission effectively found that management at Esso had not demonstrated an uncompromising commitment to identify and control every hazard at Longford. In short, if culture is the key to safety, then the root cause of the Longford accident was a deficiency in the safety culture of management.

An example of LTI distortion: maintenance

The issue of maintenance provides an important illustration of the subtle way in which Esso's focus on LTIs distracted attention from the risk of major accident.

Maintenance staff had been progressively reduced at Longford, over the period from 1992 to 1998, as a cost-cutting measure. Operators were told that maintenance cuts would continue "until they hurt". This meant that routinely there was a backlog of work orders – items which had been reported and were waiting to be repaired. To deal with this Esso had introduced a system for deciding an order of priority. People who reported matters in need of repair had to assess the urgency of the matter and assign a risk assessment number. Priority one meant urgent, to be done immediately; priority two meant the work should be done within 15 days (Dawson, 3.16). Guidelines for risk assessment indicated that top priority was to be accorded to matters which might affect the environment (pollution), production (for instance breakdowns which might result in gas going "off spec") or safety. The significance of this last category will become apparent shortly. Other matters received lower priority. Matters which workers assessed as safety-related were reviewed at a daily plant management meeting which could change the priority if it disagreed with the original assessment. According to one witness, priorities were often downgraded at these meetings.

Workers resented this system. They resented, in particular, the fact that items which they regarded as a high priority to fix might not be so regarded by the management committee. Where an automatic device failed and there were alternative manual procedures available, maintenance would be given a low priority and the device might remain out of action for long periods. But manual procedures could mean considerable extra work for the operators concerned. The only way workers could get a matter attended to quickly was to convince management that it fitted one of the priority categories. According to one operator, getting repairs done on equipment that directly affected your own workload depended on how persuasively you could argue the case for priority treatment.

The people who have the gift of the gab tend to get their work orders done but other people who aren't as good have problems. Everything that doesn't get done can and does increase our workload. That is, affects our efficiency. The frustration tends to cause people to not bother putting work orders in any more. They just forget about it. I would guess that 80% of operators don't do the risk assessments.

Against this background we can now consider the case of the automatically operated valve known as TRC3B. This valve enabled some control to be exercised over the condensate level referred to earlier. It will be recalled that the failure to effectively control the condensate level began the accident sequence. For some weeks prior to the accident the TRC3B valve was not functioning properly and operators had to manipulate a bypass valve manually to achieve an effect which would normally have been achieved automatically. According to one operator, the failure of the valve "created that much havoc on the panel, everyone was frustrated, nothing was being fixed".

Operators had put in a work order request two weeks prior to the accident but had failed to get a top priority rating for the job because the failure of TRC3B was not regarded as a safety issue.

Although the failure of the TRC3B was not regarded as having safety implications it was relevant to the accident in the following way. Because the valve was not working properly, operators had to make manual adjustments to the bypass valve continually. As described in the previous chapter, a communication failure at the shift change immediately before the accident meant that operators on the fatal shift did not carry out these adjustments in an appropriate way. This failure resulted in the spill-over of condensate into other parts of the system which initiated the accident sequence. Had the maintenance on TRC3B been done as a top priority, the valve would have been operating automatically in the shifts prior to the explosion. This would have meant that the level of condensate was more effectively controlled, making the accident sequence less likely to get under way.

The Commission was unwilling to regard the failure to repair the valve as a cause of the accident, but it conceded that it contributed "in an indirect way" (Dawson, 15.7). It is not clear exactly what the Commission meant by this phrase. Possibly it meant that, while the maintenance problem was one of the circumstances that allowed the accident to occur, it was too remote in the causal sequence to be accorded much significance. Nevertheless, it is reasonable to conclude that *but for* the failure to repair the valve, the accident would probably not have occurred. In short, the failure to give a top priority rating to the repair of the valve was one of the many "but for" causes of the accident.

Consider, finally, the way understandings about safety were involved in determining maintenance priorities. It is now apparent that the TCR3B valve was safety-relevant. Indeed, one expert witness at the inquiry argued that it was "critical ... to the safe operation of the plant". But, as this expert also noted, there was no "real understanding within Esso of the criticality". Given the inadequacy of Esso's knowledge on this point, there is no way operators or their immediate superiors could have been expected to understand the implications for safety of the breakdown of TRC3B or any similar device. Recognising the hazards posed by such breakdowns might well require a full-scale HAZOP. In short, apart from certain equipment which was explicitly defined as safety-relevant, operators were not in a position to make judgments about the significance of maintenance work for *plant* safety. They were nevertheless expected to make judgments about safety in order to fill out a work order. The only hazards they might reasonably be expected to be aware of were low intensity hazards of the sort which might result in lost-time injuries (slips, trips and falls). Equipment breakdowns seldom generated such hazards and hence operators were seldom in a position to claim that maintenance was necessary for safety reasons.

To summarise, Esso's maintenance cutbacks had generated a maintenance backlog problem which made it necessary to introduce a prioritisation process. This involved a risk assessment to establish how urgent the matter was. The way safety was understood at Esso necessarily influenced the maintenance risk assessment process, with the result that maintenance which might have been necessary from a plant safety point of view ended up with a low priority, thus endangering the plant. This is exactly what happened in the case of TRC3B. (For another example see Dawson, 13.147.)

Conclusion

I began this chapter by asking why it was that Esso's incident-reporting system systematically ignored process upsets which might have provided warnings of disaster and was used instead as a tool to prevent lost-time injuries. The answer now is obvious. Safety was measured in terms of lost-time injuries and Esso's safety efforts were therefore focused on minimising the number of minor injuries. Among other things, this resulted in an effort to create a safety culture or mindset which would encourage workers to behave more carefully. Such a strategy ignored completely the special role of management in controlling major hazards. I have also argued that the focus on lost-time injuries impeded the recognition of hazards implicit in unrepaired equipment, thereby distorting Esso's maintenance program.

All of this points to the need for alternative indicators of safety which will have a real bearing on how well major hazards are being managed. The nuclear industry in the United States has shown the way in this respect. There is no reason why other high-risk industries such as petroleum production and refining could not follow suit.

Chapter

7

Auditing

One of the central conclusions of most disaster inquiries is that the auditing of safety management systems was defective. Following the fire on the Piper Alpha oil platform in the North Sea in 1987 in which 167 men died, the official inquiry found numerous defects in the safety management system which had not been picked up in company auditing. There had been plenty of auditing, but as Appleton, one of the assessors on the inquiry, said, "it was not the right quality, as otherwise it would have picked up beforehand many of the deficiencies which emerged in the inquiry" (1994:182). Audits on Piper Alpha regularly conveyed the message to senior management that all was well. In the widely available video of a lecture on the Piper Alpha disaster Appleton makes the following comment:

> *When we asked senior management why they didn't know about the many failings uncovered by the inquiry, one of them said: "I knew everything was all right because I never got any reports of things being wrong". In my experience* [Appleton said], ... *there is always news on safety and some of it will be bad news. Continuous good news – you worry.*

Appleton's comment is a restatement of the well-known problem that bad news does not travel easily up the corporate hierarchy. High quality auditing must find ways to overcome this problem.

Esso auditing

Evidence was given at the Royal Commission that Esso's auditing process was defective in the very same way that auditing at Piper Alpha was. Just six months prior to the explosion, Esso's health and safety management system (called OIMS – Operational Integrity Management System) was audited by a team from Esso's corporate owner, Exxon. The auditing team was presumed to have an arm's length relationship with Esso and therefore to be in a position to provide an accurate evaluation of the system. Longford was one of about 11 sites in Victoria visited by the auditing team. Esso's managing director reported to the inquiry that the audit had shown that most elements of the safety management system were functioning at level three or better which meant that:

- the system is functioning;
- procedures for key tasks are documented;
- adjustments to system process steps have been made to ensure completeness and to ensure the system is functioning as intended;
- ongoing verification measures indicate that the system is working as intended;
- results and outputs are being measured; and
- priority system objectives are satisfied.

Several other elements of the safety system were assessed at level four, the highest assessment level. The managing director went on to tell the inquiry that:

since the assessment is conducted by personnel external to Esso, I felt confident that these results represented an independent and unbiased assessment of the state of Esso's OIMS systems.

He also noted that an internal review in May 1998, four months before the explosion, "highlighted a number of positive results", among them, six months without any recordable injuries ... high levels of near-miss reporting ... and major risk reduction projects".

Taken at face value these statements indicate that the reports being received at the most senior level of the corporation contained consistently goods news. This is precisely the situation which led Appleton to say: "Continuous good news – you worry".

Various parties represented at the inquiry commented privately that these statements from Esso were to be expected, that the good news story was for public consumption, and that Esso's managing director knew better.

But the evidence does not support this interpretation. Documents presented to the inquiry reveal that these same good news stories had been told to the managing director by his staff prior to the explosion. Esso's executive committee, including its directors, met periodically as a "corporate health, safety and environment committee". The results of the external audit had been presented to this committee two months prior to the explosion. The meeting was expected to take two hours and the agenda shows that just thirty minutes were allocated for a presentation to this committee about the external audit. The presentation consisted of a slide show and commentary. It included an "overview of positive findings" followed by a list of remaining "challenges". The minutes of this meeting record that the audit:

> concluded that OIMS was extensively utilized and well understood within Esso and identified a number of Exxon best practices within Esso. Improvement opportunities focussed on enhancing system documentation and formalising systems for elements 1 and 7.

Notice that the "challenges" mentioned by the presenter have become "improvement opportunities" in the minutes. Moreover, these challenges/opportunities seem to be about perfecting the system, not about ensuring that it is implemented. There is certainly no bad news here.

But the important point to note is that the good news story told by the managing director to the inquiry was not just concocted for the purposes of the inquiry, as the cynics suggested. This was the story which he had been told prior to the explosion. The audit reports coming to him were telling him essentially that all was well.

Note also that the meeting minutes describe this half-hour period as a presentation of findings to the executive committee. There is no indication that executive committee members probed these findings in any detail, nor made any decisions or issued any directions as a result of what they were told. The committee is portrayed in the minutes as a fairly passive recipient of a summary report, not as a group of directors and managers actively controlling safety in their company.

Earlier chapters have already described some of the bad news which a good audit might have been expected to pick up. First, although accident investigators quickly highlighted the fact that a HAZOP had not been carried out on gas plant 1, the external audit failed to notice this.

Second, it was no secret that operators had grown accustomed to managing the plant for long periods without responding to alarms triggered by abnormal circumstances. A thorough-going audit should have detected this. The external assessment did not. Instead, it concluded that "there was a good understanding of and high discipline in safe work routines and procedures" (Dawson, 13.36).

Third, a thorough audit should have picked up the fact that the near miss reporting system was not being used to report significant gas processing problems. The Exxon audit did not pick this up. Instead, it concluded that "near-miss reporting was actively encouraged by management and supported by Esso personnel" (Dawson, 13.36).

These are only some of the failures which became obvious during the inquiry which a thorough audit should have identified. It is clear that there was plenty of bad news around, plenty of news which, had it reached the highest levels of the company and been acted on, would have averted the incident. But the Exxon audit missed it all.

It was not just that the audit missed things it should have picked up; its principal conclusion was wrong. Remember that the central finding of the audit, as summed up in the executive committee minutes was that "OIMS (the company's safety management system) was extensively utilized and well understood within Esso". The Commission found otherwise:

> OIMS, together with all the supporting manuals, comprised a complex management system. It was repetitive, circular, and contained unnecessary cross-referencing. Much of its language was impenetrable. These characteristics made the system difficult to comprehend by management and by operations personnel.

The Commission gained the distinct impression that there was a tendency for the administration of OIMS to take on a life of its own, divorced from operations in the field. Indeed it seemed that in some respects, concentration upon the development and maintenance of the system diverted attention from what was actually happening in the practical functioning of the plants at Longford (Dawson, 13.39-40).

The Commission stated that it "can only conclude that the methodology employed by the assessment team was flawed" (Dawson, 13.37). This was not a high quality audit and its effect was to lull management into a false sense of security.

Auditing at BHP Coal

It is worth contrasting the Esso audit with an audit done by BHP Coal in Queensland in 1996, in the *aftermath* of the 1994 Moura explosion. But to set the scene we must first take note of a so-called "executive" safety audit at Moura, just three months *before* the explosion. This audit failed to identify any of the problems revealed at the Moura inquiry, and in particular, it failed to highlight the mine's systematic inattention to catastrophic risk. The audit team included a number of managers internal to BHP Coal, and, according to one BHP executive, the failure of this earlier audit was due, in part, to the unwillingness of audit team members to challenge the competence of the mine manager.

[The mine] *manager's area of responsibility is his castle. Questioning the running of this castle and especially raising issues that threaten its viability are uncomfortable* (Seymour, 1997:256).

The lesson which BHP learnt from this was the need for high-powered auditing by very senior people, organisationally remote from the site being audited. The 1996 audit was such an audit and focused on the catastrophic risk management plans at four BHP sites in Queensland. The audit team included three managers from remote parts of the BHP empire and three mining specialists from outside BHP altogether. This was a thorough-going audit which did indeed challenge managers. Seymour refers to this obliquely when he notes that the "team's reception varied considerably from site to site". At one mine for instance, the audit team discovered that the mining machines were not equipped with methane gas monitors. The mine's defence was that this was not a gassy mine and hence the monitors were unnecessary. The counter argument is that, as mining progresses into new areas, methane gas might be encountered unexpectedly, and the audit team was critical of the mine's policy on this matter. The audit team also criticised the mine for focusing on an array of minor risks, rather of catastrophic hazards.

The team presented the audit findings in detail in a half-day briefing to the chief executive officer of BHP, the parent company of BHP Coal. This presentation included what were called "key observations". Under this heading the CEO was told that "planning, process and external audit raised questions at all four sites – *serious questions at two of those sites*" (emphasis added).

The remarkable thing about this audit, then, was that it succeeded in conveying bad news to the very top of the corporate hierarchy. The summary message was not simply that all is well, but rather that things are not good enough.

BHP Coal had clearly learnt the lesson of its previous auditing failure. It had understood that the hallmark of a good audit is that it must be thorough enough to uncover the bad news about safety and convey it upwards to the top of the corporation.

The purposes of auditing

This comparison provokes some reflections on the purpose of safety auditing. It is notable that whatever else auditors say they are doing they are almost invariably on the lookout for hazards. In the case of the BHP audit described above, that was a quite explicit purpose.

The theory of safety auditing is, however, quite different. Theoretically, the aim of safety auditing is not to identify uncontrolled or inadequately controlled hazards – it is to identify strengths and weaknesses in safety management systems. This approach lends itself to providing summary evaluations of how well safety is being managed. This was the real purpose of the Exxon audit. It evaluated Esso's safety management system in relation to 11 elements and rated each on a scale of 1 to 4. The result was a score card on how well the company was managing safety. Another example of this score card approach is the five-star rating system of the National Safety Council of Australia.

This kind of evaluation serves various purposes. It enables firms to identify elements in their management systems which need attention, thus facilitating improvement. It also enables comparisons to be made, most importantly, over time. Firms can thus measure whether they are improving. Esso had external assessments done in 1994, 1997 and 1998. Based on the audit score card there was improvement between 1994 and 1997, but no overall improvement between 1997 and 1998. In fact, while some elements had improved, some had slipped back. Most notably, "risk assessment and management" had slipped from 4 in 1997 to 3 in 1998.

It is worth pointing out that an audit whose purpose is to identify hazards which have been missed does not lend itself to this score card approach. BHP's audit did not rate each site, nor did it seek to compare them. It was focused on specific catastrophic risks and probed in some detail to find out how well these risks were being managed. It asked: what kinds of things might go wrong here and what have you done to control these risks? This was an audit looking for problems. It was not a benchmarking audit to be used for comparative purposes. It is probable that audits which most effectively transmit bad news to the top of the hierarchy are audits which have abandoned any benchmarking or comparative purpose.

It may not be necessary, however, to make an either/or choice between safety system auditing and hazard identification. One of the requirements of any safety management system is that it identifies, assesses and controls hazards. A systems audit of a hazardous facility could reasonably focus on this element of the system. To rigorously assess this element, it is not enough to ask whether the company has a strategy for identifying hazards (the strategy may be inadequate) or whether it has a hazard register (the register may be incomplete). A rigorous audit needs to examine the hazard identification strategy and make some effort to seek out hazards which may have been missed, so as to be able to make a judgment about how effectively hazard identification and control is being carried out. Identifying unrecognised hazards is clearly a dramatic way of demonstrating deficiencies in management's hazard identification system. In short, even in theory it is possible for an audit which is aimed at assessing a system, to devote some effort to hazard identification. It should be noted that such an exercise cannot be done by examining a company's paperwork; it requires auditors to go into the field, looking for unrecognised problems.

Audit as challenge

Government regulators are now conducting audits on Esso's off-shore oil platforms in Bass Strait which are both system-evaluating and hazard-identifying. The strategy is to "challenge" management to demonstrate that the system is working. For example, platforms are equipped with deluge systems designed to spray large volumes of water in the event of a fire. But what assurance is there that the deluge heads are working properly? An auditor who really wants to know will not be satisfied with reports that the system has recently been checked by an outside consultant. Rather s/he will "challenge" management by asking that the system be activated. Experience elsewhere shows that such challenges are likely to reveal problems requiring corrective action. On Piper Alpha, for example, many of the deluge heads turned out to be blocked by rust.

Inspectors on Bass Strait platforms do not merely request that any problem identified be fixed. They regard the problem as an indication of something wrong with the safety management system. They will therefore request that the company attend to this *management* problem by carrying out a root cause analysis and ensuring that knowledge is transferred to other platforms. Finally, to ensure that the problem has been attended to, inspectors may check at some later date that deluge heads (to continue the example) are working on some *other* platform. This provides assurances that the management system problem has indeed been rectified, not merely that the particular deluge heads identified as defective have been fixed. This is auditing at its best, because it is aimed at uncovering both particular problems and the system defects which have allowed them to occur.

The SafetyMAP audit

Victorian WorkCover carried out an audit of Esso in 1996, two years before the explosion at Longford. Like the Exxon audit, this audit failed to uncover any of the deficiencies which led to the Longford accident. Let us consider why.

The audit tool, called SafetyMAP, was designed by WorkCover "to provide organisations with a means of measuring or 'mapping' their health and safety management systems". It is intended to be of use to large, medium and small organisations alike, and to be applicable to organisations which have only the haziest idea of how to manage safety as well as to those with highly sophisticated systems. SafetyMAP provides three levels of certification: initial, transition and advanced. "An organisation operating at Initial Level Achievement should be able to meet *basic* legislative requirements and have the *basis* for an integrated health and safety management system" (VWA, 1996:5, emphasis added). It is clear that the prerequisites for certification at the initial level are relatively modest. One significant limitation of an initial level SafetyMAP audit is that it does not investigate whether an organisation has its own auditing capacity, that is the capacity to make some assessment for itself of its safety management system. Companies with state-of-the-art management systems like OIMS might reasonably be expected to have their own internal auditing process and indeed to achieve certification at the advanced level. Yet the WorkCover audit set out to certify Esso only at the initial level. Why was this?

Esso was a self-insurer, meaning that it was not required to pay a workers' compensation insurance premium to WorkCover, and drew on its own resources to make any compensation payments to injured workers for which it was liable. Self-insurance is a privilege, not a right, granted to large companies which have the resources to cover their own workers' compensation costs and which can demonstrate to WorkCover that they are managing health and safety effectively. The SafetyMAP audit was conducted for this purpose – to certify that Esso's safety management system warranted the renewal of its self-insurer licence. It might have been thought that WorkCover would require certification at the advanced level for this purpose but, astonishingly, as a matter of policy, initial level certification was all that was required.

Here, then, is a further purpose of auditing – to provide the certification needed for self-insurance. A disclaimer in the audit report for Esso specified that this was the *only* purpose of the audit. The report explicitly stated that it "does not provide recommendations for improvement". A WorkCover witness at the inquiry confirmed this, saying that "there was no process in place for the results of these audits to be transmitted to the operational arm of the organisation ...".

Moreover, the resources devoted to the audit were strictly limited. It was carried out by two people over a period of three days, and included interviews with a number of people at Esso's Melbourne office as well as on-site interviews at Longford and at one off-shore platform, Cobia. The Longford component of the audit would therefore have taken approximately a day. Furthermore, the two auditors were "OHS management systems consultants" – they had no special expertise in the hazards of the petroleum industry.

A final comment is necessary on the verification procedures used in a SafetyMAP audit. In theory, audits must go beyond the paperwork to check whether the practice conforms to the theory. SafetyMAP manuals specify the following kinds of evidence as appropriate (emphasis added):

- *Documents* that outline the system or process being followed;

- *Records* that confirm the system or process to be followed;

- *Discussion* with personnel that indicate the system is being followed; and

- *Observations* by the auditor(s) that the system is being followed.

The first two items in this list involve paperwork verification while the third and fourth require field work.

Despite these statements of principle, SafetyMAP audits in practice rely almost exclusively on paperwork verification (see examples of verification listed in the user guide). Their ability to verify that systems are operating as intended is correspondingly limited.

Given all these limitations, there was no reason to expect that the SafetyMAP audit of Esso would be particularly searching. It would be unreasonable, therefore, to expect the auditors to have carried out a rigorous assessment of Esso's hazard identification procedures. Nevertheless, let us consider how they dealt with element 6.1.1 of SafetyMAP, namely, the requirement that "competent persons have identified potential hazards and assessed the risks arising from the work process". We know that competent persons had *not* identified the danger of cold metal embrittlement in gas plant 1. How close did the audit team get to uncovering this fact?

The audit report reveals that the auditors were provided with an immense amount of paper and were able to verify from training records that a variety of Esso personnel had received training in hazard identification and control. They also observed that there were comprehensive lists of hazards which had been identified at the two sites. But they were not in a position to evaluate the hazard identification methodologies or to investigate for themselves how complete the lists of hazards were. They certainly did not pick up the fact that gas plant 1 had never been systematically HAZOPed. Not surprisingly, they concluded in relation to element 6.1.1 of SafetyMAP that "the organisation has identified potential hazards in the workplace".

It is clear that WorkCover did not expect the SafetyMAP audit at Longford to provide a guarantee of safety. That was not its purpose. No general safety-system auditing can guarantee safety. This fact needs to be widely broadcast so that no one can be under any illusions about the significance of such audits.

Auditing to provide assurances of safety

It is interesting to compare the SafetyMAP audit at Esso with some very specific WorkCover auditing in the aftermath of the explosion, intended as far as possible to provide assurances of safety. Although gas plants 2 and 3 came back into operation less than two weeks after the accident, it was more than six months before the badly damaged gas plant 1 could be repaired and brought back into production. Prior to its recommissioning, WorkCover required Esso to do an extensive HAZOP study of the whole plant and of modifications which Esso had proposed. In order to ensure that all relevant hazards were identified and controlled, WorkCover engaged independent consultants to review the methodology used by the Esso HAZOP team and to review the HAZOP implementation process undertaken by Esso. Moreover it conducted audits to verify that Esso had done what it said it would do. In all, a total of five professionals worked on this audit process. Such high intensity auditing is a striking departure from previous WorkCover practice. There are indications that in future, more auditing of this calibre will be carried out by the new Major Hazard Unit, to be described in the next chapter.

There is an interesting idea here for companies like Esso. Perhaps major audits should aim, not simply to assess and score the operation of the safety management system, but to assure management that the facility is safe. This is a very different aim and would require a far greater expenditure of resources. Audits with this purpose would be far more likely to uncover the bad news.

Auditing the auditors

The SafetyMAP audit of Esso highlights the difficulty for a government agency in carrying out a systematic and thorough audit of the safety management system of a large hazardous operation. A more effective use of resources may be to concentrate on auditing the company's auditing procedures. This might work as follows. When company audits occur, government auditors could go in afterwards and seek to identify problems missed in the initial audit. These problems could then be regarded as indicators of defects in the company auditing procedures requiring correction. Over time this would lead to higher quality company auditing and corresponding improvements in safety management systems. It is more efficient and effective for government agencies to audit the auditors in this way than to try to audit whole safety management systems.

Conclusion

One of the findings which emerges from every disaster inquiry is that company auditing provided only good news and failed to identify problems which became very obvious after the event. At Longford, auditing by both company and government auditors failed to identify the precursors to disaster. A large scale audit which fails to uncover problems is not a credible audit. It seems reasonable to measure the success of an audit by whether or not it uncovers significant problems. This chapter has described some of the characteristics of higher quality auditing and there are indications that Victorian government auditing of hazardous industries in the post-Longford era will be of this higher quality.

Chapter

8

The Regulatory Environment

The move to self-regulation of occupational health and safety has generated considerable concern in some quarters. The Royal Commission echoed this concern. It found that the self-regulatory regime in place at Longford contributed to the accident (Dawson, 14.33) and it made detailed recommendations about an alternative regime which would most probably have prevented the explosion. This chapter addresses these issues and considers in some detail the new "safety case" approach recommended by the Commission.

Self-regulation

Recent decades have seen the progressive abandonment of detailed, prescriptive regulation of occupational health and safety in favour of what is generally referred to as self-regulation. Whereas the old-style legislation required employers to comply with precise, often quite technical rules, the new style imposes an overarching requirement on employers that they provide a safe and healthy workplace for their employees, as far as practicable (Gunningham and Johnstone, 1999). Failure to do so can result in prosecution and substantial penalties. The new legislation specifies the desired outcome but it does not tell employers what they must do to achieve that outcome. For this reason it is often described as performance-based or goal-setting legislation. The authorities may provide codes of practice to assist employers to meet their goals, but these are not mandatory.

There is no logical reason why self-regulation should be associated with a reduced level of inspection by government authorities. It is true that the removal of prescriptive requirements means the abolition of one of the previous functions of inspectors – the identification of rule violations. But inspectors are still in a position to identify ways in which employers may be failing to provide a safe workplace and to issue prohibition or improvement notices in relation to these matters. Despite this logic, the move to self-regulation has sometimes been accompanied by a reduction in resources provided for inspection and thus a reduction in the level of oversight by government agencies. Evidence was given at the inquiry that there had been a decline in the number of inspections at Longford since the repeal of the prescriptive *Boiler and Pressure Vessel Act* and associated regulations in 1995.

It needs to be noted, however, that any reduction in frequency of inspections which may have occurred at Longford cannot be regarded as having contributed to the accident. WorkCover inspectors did not have the expertise to identify hazards in technically complex plants and no matter how intensively they inspected the Longford site they could not have been expected to identify the problems which led to the explosion. It was admitted at the inquiry that inspectors were simply "out-gunned" by company experts. The regulatory regime was one which drew no distinction between the regulation of a petrochemical facility and a dry-cleaning shop, and it was this, rather than the number of inspections, that accounts for WorkCover's inability to exercise effective oversight at the Longford plant.

In principle, self-regulation is quite distinct from deregulation. The latter involves a retreat by government and an abandonment of the field to the market. Self-regulation differs from this in two fundamental respects. First, although it is up to the enterprise to work out how to achieve a safe workplace, governments provide a legislative framework to achieve this outcome and remain willing to take enforcement action as necessary. For this reason, some authors prefer to describe the process as co-regulation, involving both government and enterprise (Emmett, 1992:295). Second, employees are an integral part of any enterprise and *self*-regulation therefore requires active employee participation.

While self-regulation and deregulation are quite distinct in principle, it is clear that without active employee involvement and without a commitment by the State to ensuring safe outcomes, self-regulation runs the risk of degenerating into deregulation. This is what unions fear has happened in Australia, particularly in recent years in Victoria. Here for instance are the words of a senior OHS officer with the Victorian Trades Hall Council (Towler, 1997):

By shutting down these external controls governments have created a void in safety. When performance-based standards are introduced in conjunction with a withdrawal of government services and the political withdrawal of support for employee participation the result is a deregulation of essential safety arrangements.

Another union safety official makes the point in this way: "on sites without union involvement, the application of performance-based laws ... is often perceived to mean deregulation" (Berger, 1999b:63). Workers who might tentatively propose to their employer that perhaps a truck needs a reversing beeper or that a guard should be 90 cms high are likely to be told, rightly or wrongly, that there are no longer any such requirements and that it all depends on whether the employer thinks it's safe enough (Berger, 1999b:62).

Self-regulation is often assumed to be the optimal regulatory style for large employers who have their own health and safety expertise. For such employers, it is argued, the removal of detailed prescriptive constraints provides them with the freedom to choose the best strategies for achieving safety in their particular context (Glen, 1993). In the case of small employers, however, it is commonly argued that self-regulation is problematic (Lamm, 1999). Most small business operators resent the uncertainty involved. They want to be told precisely what to do so that they can do it and get on with the job, secure in the knowledge that they have complied with their obligations.

Interestingly, the findings of the Royal Commission call into question whether the regime of self-regulation which has developed in Australia in recent years is optimal even for large employers. The presumption is that self-regulation allows large companies to implement best practice. The Commission found, to the contrary, that self-regulation at Longford allowed Esso to fall considerably short of best practice and it concluded that:

external obligations of a detailed and comprehensive kind (albeit identified by Esso itself) should be imposed upon Esso in order to avoid the repetition of an accident such as occurred on [25 September 1998] (Dawson, 15.14).

The reasoning was as follows. Best practice hazard identification would have involved carrying out a HAZOP of gas plant 1. Esso did not carry out such a HAZOP and defended itself by arguing that it was not required to do so, either by law or under Exxon's own guidelines. Had it been operating under the more stringent safety case regime, to be discussed in the next section, it would probably have been required to carry out such a HAZOP. Ironically, recent legislation had imposed safety case regimes, both upstream of Longford, on Esso's oil platforms in Bass Strait, and downstream of Longford, on the operators of the gas pipeline. In short, although best practice was in the process of being implemented both upstream and downstream, it was not being implemented at Longford itself because it was not legally required.

The origins of the safety case regime

The safety case approach recommended by the Royal Commission had its origins in Europe in the 1970s. In 1974 an explosion in a chemical plant at Flixborough in the UK killed 28 men and caused extensive damage and injuries in surrounding villages. In 1976 an accidental release of a toxic chemical from a plant at Seveso in Italy caused burns and skin problems to 700 people in a nearby village. These two accidents led European authorities to decide that a new approach to safety was necessary for controlling major hazards in industries with the potential for disaster which went beyond the factory gates. Self-regulatory strategies were not enough and new controls were needed. It was a decade however before the new safety case approach was finally adopted in the European Community – the Seveso directive. In the UK this new approach was embodied in the CIMAH (Control of Industrial Major Accident Hazards) Regulations which became law in 1984 (Kletz, 1994:81). The safety case regime was adopted for offshore petroleum production in the UK following the Piper Alpha disaster of 1988.

There is some evidence to suggest that the introduction of safety case requirements in Europe has curbed the rate of major accidents. From

1952 the rate rose almost exponentially to a total of 99 in the seven-year period 1973-79. In the next seven-year period the number of major accidents declined to 66. The decline coincides with the development and implementation of the Seveso directive (NOHSC, 1996b:19).

In Australia the safety case strategy was adopted in 1993 for the offshore oil and gas industry (DPIE, 1995). As for major hazards *onshore*, following an explosion in a chemical factory at St Peters, Sydney in 1990 and a fire at a chemical tank farm at Coode Island, Melbourne in 1991, the National Occupational Health and Safety Commission (NOHSC) began work on a model for safety case legislation which it published in 1996. The hope was that the various states would adopt the model, but only Western Australia had done so prior to the Longford explosion. At the time of writing, Victoria had drafted major hazard facilities regulations, and was moving rapidly towards developing a safety case regime.

What is a safety case?

The essence of the new approach is that the operator of a major hazard installation is required to *make a case* or *demonstrate* to the relevant authority that safety is being or will be effectively managed at the installation. Whereas under the self-regulatory approach, the facility operator is normally left to its own devices in deciding how to manage safety, under the safety case approach it must lay out its procedures for examination by the regulatory authority. This is a major departure from previous practice.

Just what must be included in the safety case varies from one jurisdiction to another. But one core element in all cases is the requirement that facility operators systematically identify all major incidents that could occur, assess their possible consequences and likelihood and demonstrate that they have put in place appropriate control measures as well as appropriate emergency procedures. All this sounds like the standard requirement that hazards be identified, assessed and controlled. In essence it is. But the difference is that operators are required to *demonstrate* to the regulator the processes they have gone through to identify the hazards, the methodology they have used to assess the risks and the reasons why they have chosen one control measure rather than another. If this reasoning involves a cost-benefit analysis, the basis of this analysis must be laid out for scrutiny. Other elements included in safety case regimes are a specification of just what counts as a major hazard facility, a requirement that facility operators have an ongoing safety management system and the requirement that employees be involved at all stages.

The role of the regulator

What is the role of the regulatory authority once a safety case has been prepared by the facility operator? Early safety case regimes, such as that which applied onshore in the UK, simply required that the regulator receive or acknowledge the case, not necessarily that it pass any judgment on it (Barrell, 1992:7). The alternative approach is that the regulator be required to either accept or reject the case. As Barrell (1992:7) argues:

> *Acceptance constitutes an integral and logical part of the system. It would be inconsistent for the authorities to require in the Safety Case a demonstration that safety management systems are adequate, that risks to persons from major accident hazards have been reduced to the lowest level that is reasonably practicable, etc, and then not accept (or otherwise) the case presented.*

Recent safety case legislation gives the regulator this more active role of accepting or rejecting the safety case. It is significant that the regulator responsible for enforcing the offshore safety case regime in Victoria, the Department of Natural Resources and Environment (DNRE), has recently rejected 10 out of 14 safety cases submitted by Esso for its platforms in Bass Strait. They were rejected on four grounds (letter dated 15/11/99):

1. *Esso had failed to demonstrate adequate employee involvement in preparation of cases.*

2. *The decisions on which the case was based were not transparent.*

3. *Esso had failed to demonstrate a complete and proper assessment of risks.*

4. *Esso had failed to demonstrate it had reduced risks as low as reasonably practicable.*

Esso was requested to revise and resubmit its safety cases within nine months. Whereas doubts had previously been expressed in some quarters about the precise role of the offshore regulator in this matter, this decision has clarified it once and for all.

The model regulation published by NOHSC in 1996 was not clear about the role of the regulator. It stated that "the role of the relevant public authority ... includes ... *receiving* safety reports [cases] and *giving assurances* to government that an appropriate level of safety applies" (NOHSC, 1996a:22, emphasis added). Whether the authority might actually reject a case was not spelled out.

The draft Victorian major hazard facilities regulations, which draw their inspiration from the national model (VWA, 1999a:9), remove this ambiguity by requiring major hazard facilities to obtain a licence to operate, which will only be granted after the Authority has approved the safety case.

An explanatory paper issued with the draft Victorian regulations notes that "one of the principal disadvantages of licensing is that it can be perceived that the regulating agency who issues the licence, assumes legal responsibility for the licensed activity" (VWA, 1999b:12). The paper explains, however, that this assumption is wrong and that legal responsibility for the safe operation of major hazard facilities rests with the company.

The scope of the draft Victorian regulations

Following international practice the draft Victorian major hazard facilities regulations define a major hazard facility as one which contains more than specified amounts of particular dangerous substances. For the most part a dangerous substance is one which is explosive, flammable, oxidising or toxic.

There are, of course, other types of hazards which do not involve dangerous substances which nevertheless have the capacity to cause widespread death and injury, for example the hazards of air, sea and rail transport. Such hazards are not covered by the new regulations. Stimulated in part by some major accidents in the 1980s, the British rail system has operated under a safety case regime since the mid 1990s (Maidment, 1998). The question of whether mass transportation systems in Australia should operate under similar regimes has not yet been seriously raised.

The new Victorian regulations will apply to Longford itself but not upstream or downstream of Longford, where separate regulatory regimes apply.

Based on all these considerations, there are approximately 45 sites in Victoria which will be covered by the new regulations.

The new prescription

One of the interesting aspects of the emergence of safety case regimes is that they undermine the dichotomy between prescription and performance standards. Formally speaking, safety case regulation is performance or outcome oriented: the ultimate legal requirement is a safe workplace and how this is achieved is to some extent up to the employer. However, the reality is that safety cases represent a new form of prescription. The draft regulations run to 55 pages and are full of mandatory requirements. The word "must" appears frequently, six times on page 11, for example. Porter and Wettig (1999:3) describe this new approach as a " balance" between goal setting and prescription.

The new prescription differs from the old in that the old style prescribed technical requirements, while the new style prescribes how safety is to be managed. The new regulations specify, for example, what kinds of documents must be maintained, when and how often the safety management system must be reviewed, what possible consequences of major hazard incidents are to be identified, what role employees are to play, and so on.

Moreover, the new prescriptive requirements are enforceable. For instance, section 302 of the draft Victorian regulations specifies that companies must identify and document all major hazards and that failure to do so is an indictable offence. Again, once the safety case is agreed, departures from agreed practice will be liable to sanctions. The new prescription will be just as enforceable as the old.

The costs of complying with the new prescriptive requirements will be considerable. It may cost a large company up to $500,000 just to prepare the initial safety case (VWA, 1999b:25). This figure does not include the costs of control measures identified as being necessary. The new prescription is even more "burdensome", therefore, than the old. On reflection this is not surprising. It is clear that companies must expend considerable resources if catastrophic hazards are to be controlled. There is no way around this, regardless of what kind of regulatory regime is in force.

Given this discussion of the old and new prescription, the role of self-regulation in the Longford disaster can now be clarified. Certain critics have argued that the move from the old prescriptive style of legisation to self-regulation contributed to the accident at Longford. But the old prescriptive regime had not identified the long-standing problems which led to the accident and there is no reason to think that, had that regime continued, the outcome would have been different. It was not the move away from the old prescriptive style to self-regulation, but the failure to move from self-regulation towards the new prescription that was critical. It was in this sense that self-regulation can be said to have contributed to the accident.

Lessons from offshore

A safety case regime has been in operation for offshore petroleum production since the mid-1990s. It is instructive to examine the experience in Bass Strait for insights relevant to the new onshore regime.

Employee involvement

The first lesson is the importance of employee participation, demonstrated in the following account. Workers who arrive on an oil platform are routinely allocated to a rescue vehicle permanently located on the platform. In the event of an emergency they are supposed to board the vehicle which is winched down into the water and then moves away from the platform. On one occasion, in 1998, arriving workers were allocated to a vehicle when it was known that the winch was faulty and would be out of action for two or three days. A health and safety representative who had been working on a Bass Strait platform which caught fire in 1989 took up the issue. "If a workplace onshore catches fire you have a chance – you can run" he told me. "What is so terrifying about fire on an offshore platform is that there is nowhere to run." His view was that workers who could not be allocated to a rescue vehicle which was in good order should be removed from the platform until the necessary repairs had been made. Accordingly, he complained about the situation to the regulatory authority which issued a directive to Esso. This was a matter which would not have come to light were it not for employee involvement.

The Department of Natural Resources and Environment (DNRE) has not always been sympathetic to union initiatives. In December 1998 health and safety representatives presented a list of 18 concerns to the DNRE. One was as follows. After the Longford explosion on 25 September 1998, Bass Strait platforms attempted to close certain valves in order to stop the flow of oil and gas ashore which, it was feared, might feed the Longford fire. However one of the valves failed to close and several others did not close properly. This was a serious safety failure. Employee representatives were not convinced that the problem had subsequently been adequately dealt with and listed this as one of their concerns. The Department's response was terse and somewhat dismissive. All the matters complained of were either under control, too general to be responded to, or matters "totally within the ability and responsibility of platform crew to control". Its view was that there were no outstanding hazards on the platforms (letter, 7/12/98).

More recently the Department has reaffirmed the importance of employee involvement in a very tangible way. It issued a directive to Esso that employees be involved in a risk assessment concerning emergency evacuation vehicles. Furthermore, as already noted, one of the grounds for refusing to accept Esso's safety cases was the failure to demonstrate employee involvement.

The draft Victorian major hazard facilities regulations place considerable stress on employee involvement. The offshore experience shows the wisdom of this approach.

Conflict of interest

A second issue which the offshore regime raises is the possibility that a regulatory authority might be caught in a conflict of interest. The DNRE is responsible for encouraging the development of the State's natural resources. At the same time it is responsible for ensuring offshore safety, which may involve imposing considerable costs on facility operators and occasionally interrupting production.

This issue came to a head following the Piper Alpha disaster. The regulator at that time was the Department of Energy, responsible for both safety and production. The inquiry found that this had seriously compromised the Department's capacity to regulate safety and recommended that the safety function be removed from the Department and vested in the British Health and Safety Executive, which has country-wide responsibility for safety and no brief for production (Cullen, 1990:392).

In Australia, the federal government oversees the State authorities which deal with offshore petroleum production. A recent paper prepared by the federal department which carries out this function (the Department of Industry Science and Resources) recognises that there is a "potential conflict of interest between regulation and facilitation of resource development" and raises the question of how this can best be managed (DISR, 1999).

There is some evidence that this conflict has not been optimally managed in Victoria in the past. Bass Strait safety cases were originally required to be presented to the regulator in July 1996, unless otherwise approved. The DNRE apparently approved delays totalling three years, since the cases were only finally submitted in 1999. This relatively relaxed approach by the regulator meant that safety throughout this period remained correspondingly compromised. On the other hand, the fact that the DNRE rejected most of the cases when they were finally submitted suggests that it is now managing the potential conflict in new ways. Certainly Esso feels that, all of a sudden, the rules of the game have changed.

Resources

Another issue which has been raised about the off-shore regulatory regime is the adequacy of resources available to the DNRE. The DSIR paper makes the following point.

> *An observation that has emerged from* [federal] *audits and which applies to most if not all jurisdictions is that the levels of regulatory resources available to administer the safety case regime are barely adequate. Just as industry faces cost pressures, state and territory government departments responsible for offshore petroleum regulation operate in an environment where they are expected to do more with less. Limited resources*

*obviously have the potential to affect the degree to which a
regulator can test a safety case and verify its implementation.*

The next sections take up these issues of potential conflict of interest
and adequacy of resourcing in relation to the Major Hazards Unit
which will have the job of administering the new Victorian regulations.

The potential conflict of interest

The Royal Commission recommended the creation of a Major Hazards
Unit to administer the new safety case regime. Even before the
Commission report appeared, the Victorian WorkCover Authority
(VWA) had taken various initiatives aimed at setting up such a unit
within the VWA. The Commission made the following comment:

*It has been suggested that there is a conflict of interest between
the role of the VWA with respect to accident compensation and its
role as the supervisor of workplace safety regimes. The
Commission is in no position to reach a conclusion whether such
a conflict exists, but it is clear that if there is to be a Major
Hazard Unit within the VWA, it should be given the independence
necessary to ensure that any conflict is eliminated* (Dawson,
14.41).

The Victorian government was initially sympathetic to this concern.
The Premier announced that the Unit would need to be set up
separately. Otherwise, he said, there could be a "potential perception of
conflict" between the Authority's dual roles of prosecuting employers
for breaching workplace safety and administering accident
compensation to workers (*The Age*, 6/7/99). Shortly afterwards the
Premier reversed his position and announced that the new Unit would
be located within WorkCover (*The Age*, 15/8/99).

The potential for a conflict between the VWA's roles of accident
compensation and accident prevention is less obvious than the
production/safety conflict which the DNRE must manage and requires
some explanation.

In its role as workers' compensation insurer, VWA functions in some
respects like any insurance company. It receives premiums from
employers, who in this sense are the VWA's clients. The Authority is
under constant pressure to reduce premiums charged to its clients and
its overwhelming concern is sound financial management of the

enormous fund which it controls. On the other hand, the VWA administers legislation aimed at preventing injury and illness, such as the *Occupational Health and Safety Act* and the *Dangerous Goods Act*. The obligations under these Acts fall largely on employers and exist for the protection of workers. In this sense it is the workers who are the clients of the VWA. Furthermore, the interests of these client groups do not always coincide. This is the structural origin of the potential conflict of interest in which any organisation responsible for both workers' compensation and the enforcement of accident prevention legislation finds itself. Moreover, because financial performance is so important, there is a risk that fund management concerns will take priority over prevention or enforcement whenever a choice between the two has to be made.

The potential for conflict of interest can be brought home by considering the question of whose side a compensation/enforcement agency is on when a worker sues an employer for common law negligence, in jurisdictions where this is possible. In general the insurer stands behind the employer in such circumstances and indemnifies the employer against damages. On the other hand the injury may have resulted from a violation of some safety regulation, in which case the enforcement arm may be seeking to prosecute the company. Enforcement and compensation are thus at loggerheads. Enforcement personnel may demand information from the company for use in a case against it, while the compensation arm will have an interest in suppressing any information which might demonstrate company negligence. There is thus a potential tussle over ownership of information. There is also the possibility, in theory, that where very large damages are at stake, or the matter is precedent-setting, a board which is oriented to the protection of the fund might bring some pressure to bear on the prosecutorial arm of the agency not to proceed. There may, of course, be organisational ways of protecting the prosecution division against such pressure, but the risk remains that if the stakes are high enough subtle ways will be found to bring such pressure to bear.

At the time of writing, the situation described above cannot occur in Victoria since there is currently no common law right to sue. Should common law rights be reintroduced this particular conflict of interest will again become a theoretical possibility. I am not suggesting that this is a problem which routinely bedevils compensation/enforcement authorities when common law rights exist. I present this scenario simply because it highlights so strikingly the possibility of conflict of interest.

The critical importance of fund protection for organisations such as the VWA poses another more subtle and more pervasive danger. It is that the inspectorate will find itself harnessed to the task of reducing compensation costs rather than enforcing laws designed to control hazards. Compensation costs are driven by lost-time injury claims and WorkCover-type organisations naturally direct their efforts to industries where claims are high. If such tendencies go unchecked this can lead to a loss of focus on matters which, though serious, generate relatively few claims. For example, hazardous substances which cause long latency period diseases, such as cancer, do not generate substantial numbers of claims. Or again, major hazards which have the potential to cause catastrophic events if not properly identified and controlled may not generate lost-time injuries in the normal course of events. An agency driven by compensation concerns alone will tend to ignore such matters (see further, Hopkins, 1995, chap 12).

Enough has been said to indicate that this issue of priority-setting involves an inherent conflict of interest which an organisation like the VWA must find ways to manage. It is beyond the scope of this book to make any overall judgment about how well the VWA has performed in this respect. Nevertheless, it is reasonable to conclude that the VWA's failure to secure the implementation of the 1996 national model for the control of major hazard facilities, or to set up a specialist major hazard unit, until faced with the Longford crisis, is evidence of a tendency to focus on the high frequency, relatively low consequence events, which generate the bulk of compensation claims, at the expense of low frequency, high consequence events which generate very few. Given that companies in major hazard industries tend to display this very tendency, it is vital that government agencies are set up in such a way as to counteract it.

As mentioned earlier, Western Australia had adopted the national model *prior* to the Longford explosion. Queensland had also begun drafting the necessary legislation before the accident. It is probably not coincidental that in both states the OHS enforcement agency has remained separate from the workers' compensation administration. Note, too, that the national model was the outcome of an initiative taken by the now defunct Victorian OHS Authority which produced draft regulations in 1991 for consideration by the National Occupational Health and Safety Commission. At the time of this 1991 initiative, the administration of compensation and OHS legislation was separate in Victoria and the Victorian OHS Authority had no compensation responsibilities. This agency was still promoting what was by this time the *draft* national model in 1995. When the two organisations merged in 1996 the impetus to implement the national model waned. It would appear that the separation of responsibilities prior to 1996 facilitated a sharper focus on major hazards than was possible after the OHS agency was incorporated into VWA.

This is the background to the question of whether VWA is the best location for the Major Hazard Unit which will administer the new regulations. It may be that the Unit can be set up within WorkCover in such a way as to quarantine it from any possible conflicts. But there is another model which is worth considering – the Health and Safety Executive in the UK. This agency has no workers' compensation role but administers health and safety legislation in a variety of contexts. It is responsible not only for general occupational health and safety legislation but also for the safety case regimes for hazardous facilities, both onshore and offshore. Moreover, it administers the British railway safety case regime. A super safety agency in Victoria, incorporating the new Major Hazard Unit, the safety arm of the Department of Natural Resources and Environment and certain other safety agencies is a model which would remove altogether the need to manage the potential conflicts of interest identified in this chapter.

Another model would be to set up the Major Hazard Unit on a national basis. This is the recommendation of a recent report to NOHSC:

> *More than any other area of OHS regulation in Australia, we consider that there is a strong case for the creation of an independent and national Authority to oversee the implementation and enforcement of a national scheme for the regulation of major hazard facilities* (Gunningham, et al, 1999:6).

Such a national authority could take over the administration of offshore safety as well as other national regulatory responsibilities.

The resourcing issue

The final lesson from the offshore experience is the need for adequate resourcing of the Major Hazard Unit, wherever it may be located. Consider, for a moment, the US experience in relation to the most hazardous of all industries – nuclear power generation. The regulatory regime in the US involves inspections/audits of particular sites by teams of up to 20 inspectors working for two weeks on site. The regulator also has a policy of placing two "resident inspectors" on site full time, for long periods (Rees, 1994:33-4, 54). The policy of resident inspectors was used in US coal mines in the 1970s for mines with the worst accident records. As a result, the fatality rates at these mines fell almost immediately to well below the national average (Braithwaite, 1985). It is hard to imagine any government in Australia resourcing inspectorates in such a way as to make this possible, but these are benchmarks which should be borne in mind.

WorkCover's Major Hazard Unit envisages a staff of eight technical specialists to be responsible for about 45 facilities. This level of resourcing does not permit the intensity of scrutiny which occurs in the nuclear industry in the US. Perhaps this is inevitable, given the relative risks involved. Moreover, numbers are not everything. The quality of staff is crucially important and a WorkCover advertisement for the new positions (*The Age*, 8/5/99) indicates that the staff of the new unit will be very highly qualified for administering the new safety case regime.

Conclusion

This chapter has identified the nature of the regulatory regime in place at Longford as a factor contributing to the accident. The regime in question had evolved in recent years in a self-regulatory direction and it allowed Esso to operate the Longford facility in a manner which fell short of industry best practice. The Commission recommended that the existing regime be replaced with a safety case approach which would prescribe in detail how safety was to be managed at major hazard facilities. The central feature of the approach is that facility operators are required to *demonstrate* to the authorities that they are managing safety effectively. Had such a regime been in place at Longford, the view of the Commission was that "it is very likely that [Esso] would have identified the hazards which were in evidence on that day"

(Dawson, 14.33). These findings support the disquiet felt by many about the risks inherent in a purely self-regulatory approach to safety.

The Victorian government has accepted the Commission's recommendations and the safety case regime will be administered by a Major Hazards Unit. It is proposed that the new unit be located within the Victorian WorkCover Authority. This chapter has argued that there is a conflict of interest inherent in the operations of the Victorian WorkCover Authority which may explain the relative lack of attention which the Authority paid to major hazard facilities prior to the Longford explosion. The question therefore arises as to whether the VWA is the best location for the new Unit. The Commission expressed the view that the Major Hazards Unit should be "sufficiently independent of the VWA to avoid any conflict of interest" (Dawson, 15.26). VWA may well be able to manage the potential conflict successfully, but an alternative model which deserves consideration is the establishment of a health and safety authority modelled on the British Health and Safety Executive. There is a good case for setting this up on a national basis.

Chapter

9

Privatisation

"The current culture of privatisation and deregulation contributed to the disaster." This was one of the principal submissions to the Royal Commission by the then Labor opposition in the State Parliament. The submission was primarily concerned with the privatisation of the State's gas transmission system and claimed, in particular, that:

the Victorian government's focus on the privatisation of the gas industry distracted it from properly considering security of supply issues and this left Victorians more vulnerable in the event of major supply disruptions.

This is an intriguing claim in that it pinpoints the ideological orientation of the government of the day as the ultimate source of the problem. This chapter sets out to explore the claim that privatisation can be considered one of the root causes of the disaster.

Privatisation of urban services

Prior to 1994 gas distribution and marketing in Victoria was in the hands of a single, government-owned entity, the Gas and Fuel Corporation of Victoria. The privatisation of such an entity is a complex process. It cannot be simply sold off, for that would create a private monopoly which all sides of politics agree would be detrimental to consumers. Instead, the enterprise must first be "unbundled", to use one of the jargon words of the Victorian gas industry, split into its various components, which must be "ring-fenced", to use another vogue word, and required to operate as far as possible on a commercial basis. An important part of this "unbundling" is to split the service into geographic regions. Setting up these entities as market driven organisations is known as corporatisation. Once corporatised they can then be sold to private owners – privatised. Privatisation is thus the end point of a protracted process of restructuring. But to simplify discussion the process in its entirety will be referred to here as privatisation.

The privatisation of urban services such as gas, electricity, water, rail and bus transport has been occurring in a number of countries, including Australia, over the last couple of decades. The sell-off of government-owned entities has been driven in part by a belief that privately owned enterprises are more efficient in some sense than those which are publicly owned. But the process has given rise to widespread concern that the reliability and safety of these services has been sacrificed. Let us consider this matter in a wider context before focusing on the case of Victorian gas.

There are at least two ways in which privatisation might threaten reliability and safety. The first is that the goal of profit making will take precedence over all other considerations, and the second is that the fragmentation of service will lead to problems of coordination at the interfaces of the privatised entities.

In relation to the first, there is considerable overseas evidence that privatisation is followed by cutbacks in maintenance in order to reduce costs and that this in turn leads to an increase in supply interruptions (Quiggin, et al, 1998;51-5; Neutze, 1997:227-31). The privatisation of the British rail system in the early 1990s, for instance, has had demonstrable effects on reliability of service (*Guardian Weekly*, 11/4/99).

Moreover, privatised organisations may decide explicitly against safety-related spending, unless governments are willing to foot the bill. Writing in 1996 about the corporatised Sydney Water, Neutze noted that:

Sydney Water is only willing and in some respects only able to introduce new measures to reduce the damage its effluent causes to the environment if the government decides that it should do so and is willing to fund the measures ... The same is true in relation to the additional water treatment required to reduce the risk of water borne disease. It is ironic that the core responsibilities of Sydney Water Corporation, to supply safe water and to protect the environment, have come to be regarded as optional additions to its responsibilities, to be funded separately (Neutze, 1996:19-20).

The case of Sydney Water also illustrates the problem of fragmentation of responsibility for safety. Cryptosporidium bacteria were found in the water supply in 1998 leading to a major health scare. While the Sydney Water Corporation was publicly owned, the Prospect water filtration plant was privately operated. The contract under which it operated had not specified that the operator should monitor for giardia and cryptosporidium (Hopkins, 1999:32). So it didn't. The bacteria were not detected prior to distribution to Sydney suburbs and residents were forced to boil their drinking water for weeks. Safety in this matter had fallen through the cracks of the partially privatised system.

This problem of managing the organisational interfaces is regarded as the single biggest safety issue for the British rail system. Failure to manage this interface adequately was identified as one of the root causes of the Clapham railway accident in 1988 in the UK in which 35 people died and 500 were injured (Maidment, 1998:228; Kletz, 1994:194). Moreover, as part of the process of privatisation the track maintenance arm of British Rail was split into a number of regional companies. Poor coordination between these companies was responsible for at least two dangerous incidents and a high level of non-compliance with agreed safe systems of work (Maidment, 1998:229).

This discussion is in no way definitive. It serves simply to provide background to the hypothesis that privatisation of Victoria's gas system may have had some detrimental consequences. This hypothesis will be explored in what follows.

The privatisation of Victoria's gas transmission system

Victoria's gas is privately produced. But, until 1994, it was distributed and marketed by a government-owned entity, the Gas and Fuel Corporation. In 1994 the Kennett Liberal government split the Gas and Fuel Corporation into a gas transmission pipelines operation, the Gas Transmission Corporation, and a distribution and marketing organisation known as Gascor. This latter entity was split in 1997 into three distribution and three retail entities, which were subsequently sold. There were thus seven new companies doing what had formerly been done by one. To manage this diversity, the government established two new government entities. One of these, the Office of Gas Safety, is responsible for ensuring that the gas distribution system operates safely. It is not responsible for safety at Longford, or at upstream production sites. The other government entity, VENCorp, manages the whole distribution system. VENCorp interfaces with Longford and places the daily gas order which Esso must fill.

Did privatisation contribute to the explosion?

The accident at Longford which killed two men and injured eight others was a tragedy for those concerned. However, it was the interruption of supply from Longford which really impacted on Victorians. Longford supplied 98 per cent of Victoria's gas needs and the fact that Longford was out of action for two weeks meant that the State was without gas for two weeks. Gas is the primary energy source in Victoria for 80 per cent of residential households (Collins, 1999:4), 50 per cent of commercial enterprises and 25 per cent of industrial enterprises. The loss of gas supply therefore caused physical and/or economic hardship to the great majority of Victorians.

This analysis suggests that there are two ways in which privatisation might conceivably have contributed to the interruption of supply. The first was by contributing to the accident itself and the second was by perpetuating a system in which there was only one supplier and no back-up in the event of any supply failure.

Consider, first, the possibility that privatisation contributed to the accident itself. The opposition submission noted that VENCorp had responsibility for overseeing the gas transmission system and specifically for controlling the security of that system, but it had no responsibility for ensuring the supply from Longford. VENCorp had "responsibility only from the fence at the edge of the Longford facility" and no obligation to inspect the Longford plant. The submission reinforced the point by quoting the Treasurer's statement that "VENCorp does not, as part of its statutory functions, inspect gas production facilities". It contrasted this with the far greater breadth of responsibility exercised by the old Gas and Fuel Corporation which inspected the Longford site regularly. It should be noted, too, that because of its monolithic position the expertise available to the Gas and Fuel Corporation in carrying out these inspections was considerable.

What are we to make of this point? The conclusion which is implied, but not explicitly stated in the opposition's submission, is that had Gas and Fuel continued in existence and continued to inspect the Longford plant, the accident might have been avoided.

This is a very doubtful proposition. The problems which led to the explosion were long-standing yet had not been picked up by Gas and Fuel inspectors prior to privatisation in 1994. There is no reason to think that they would have been identified subsequently. Thus the fact that VENCorp's responsibility stopped very clearly at the fence makes no difference and the privatisation of the gas transmission system cannot reasonably be said to have contributed to the accident.

The government failure to secure supply

Consider now the second and central argument in the opposition's submission, namely, that the policy of privatisation distracted the government from the need to develop alternative sources to secure supply. There are really two claims here – that the government failed to give priority to securing alternatives and that this failure was attributable to the policy of privatisation. The first is relatively uncontentious; the second is more problematic.

In order to demonstrate the first we need only consider the government's response to the failure of supply after the Longford accident. Here are words of the relevant Minister.

> *Following the disruptions to gas supplies in 1998 – and the consequent risk to supply levels in winter 1999 – we developed a "whole of government" response strategy. This strategy includes accelerated development of a number of projects that will enhance the diversification and capacity of the system to provide security of supply. These projects include bringing forward the construction of the South West Pipeline between Port Campbell and Lara and the accelerated development of the Western Underground Gas Storage project* (McNamara, 1999:1).

The government allocated $70 million for these initiatives to ensure that the gas demand for winter 1999 could be met (Hawes, 1999:26). Three projects are of particular relevance to this discussion.

South west pipeline

A pipeline was to be constructed from the existing gas fields at Port Campbell in south western Victoria to join the State's main transmission network at Lara near Geelong. Among other things this would facilitate the development of a new offshore gas field near Port Campbell. It would also facilitate the underground storage project discussed below.

Underground gas storage

The depleted Port Campbell gas fields were to be used as a huge storage reservoir into which gas could be pumped during summer and drawn on during periods of peak demand in winter. This reservoir would hold enough gas to supply the State's needs for several days. As such it would provide an important back-up in the event of production failures.

Increasing the capacity of the link to the NSW network.

At the time there was a small capacity pipeline between Wagga and Wodonga linking Victoria to the NSW network. It was not large enough to transfer a substantial volume of gas into Victoria in the event of production failures. The capacity of this line was to be increased nearly five-fold.

These projects could all have been implemented much earlier if government policy had been focused on improving security of supply. In 1988 the Gas and Fuel Corporation recommended the construction of the underground storage facility at Port Campbell, but nothing effective had been done about this by the time of the accident. The interstate pipeline represented another missed opportunity to improve security of supply. The original intention was to spend $170 million for the construction of the pipeline. In the event only $20 million was spent and the size of the pipeline actually built in 1997/98 was much smaller than originally planned. It was able to supply only 2 per cent of Victoria's needs during the crisis, as opposed to the 30 per cent which the State opposition claimed would have been possible had the $170 million been spent.

The hydrate incident

There is one further piece of evidence of the government's lack of attention to security of supply, namely, its inadequate response to the so-called hydrate incident. In June 1998 a hydrate blockage formed in the intake lines to the Longford plant which prevented Esso from meeting the State's gas demand on 10, 11 and 14 June. The Royal Commission investigated this incident and concluded that it did not contribute in any way to the explosion on 25 September 1998. However the incident was a clear indication of the vulnerability of the gas supply.

Any government concerned about security of supply might have been expected to take this warning seriously and to take steps to ensure that such a disruption did not occur again. The State opposition requested information about the government's response, under freedom of information legislation. On the basis of the information supplied it concluded:

> *It appears that the Treasurer did not seek, nor was provided with, any advice in relation to the incident at any stage, and did not ascertain whether contingency plans existed, or should be established, for any possible future incidents.*

The effect of privatisation on security of supply

The preceding discussion demonstrates that prior to the Longford explosion the government failed to address adequately the issue of security of supply, although it would have been quite feasible for it to do so. We can conclude, therefore, that this failure contributed to the two-week interruption of supply, in the sense that, had the government seriously addressed this security of supply issue, the Longford accident would have had considerably less impact on the supply of gas to Victoria. That much of the opposition's argument seems undeniable. But the crux of the opposition's claim is that this policy failure was due to the government's privatisation agenda. Let us consider the evidence for this claim.

The government's objective, as communicated to the consultants managing the privatisation process, was as follows.

> *Within three years to have a privately owned, integrated, competitive energy sector operating on national market principles and with no residual market risk left with government.*

As the opposition submission points out, there is no mention of security of supply in this objective (p8). There is no recognition that the government might have a "residual" community service obligation to underwrite security of supply of an essential service.

The impact of the privatisation agenda can be seen very clearly in the handling of the pipeline linking Victoria and NSW. The pipeline was the responsibility of the new Gas Transmission Corporation (GTC). The 1996 annual report of the GTC explained that:

A corporate culture that results in the GTC being quick to grasp new opportunities and to be clearly focused on the commercial and financial outcomes of those opportunities is one of the Corporation's key goals (GTC, 1996:9).

It is not surprising, therefore, that the GTC saw the new pipeline as an "opportunity" for "business growth", not as a means of securing supply (GTC, 1996:8,9). It noted that "an exciting example of the project's potential (was) the likely and growing demand for gas from proposed electricity co-generation projects in NSW".

Moreover, a government statement in early 1998 spoke of the pipeline's capacity to transmit gas from south to north, further emphasising its role in facilitating new markets for Victorian gas north of the border. Since such markets would only develop slowly there was no need for a large capacity pipeline at the outset. Had the pipeline been envisaged as transmitting gas from north to south in the event of a major disruption to production in Victoria, a very different decision would have been made.

One other indication of the loss of focus on security of supply is to be found in the legislation. The legislation under which the Gas and Fuel Corporation had operated specified that one of its objectives was "to ensure the safe, economical and effective supply of gas and fuel to Victoria". Under the new regime VENCorp had no corresponding mandate to ensure supply in an overall sense; its mandate was restricted to the operation of the gas transmission system (*Gas Industry Act 1994*, section 16C). Under the new privatised arrangements, therefore, no one was even theoretically responsible for overall security of supply. This was a matter which had simply slipped through the cracks of the "unbundled" system.

The evidence therefore supports the then opposition's claim that:

the Victorian government's focus on the privatisation of the gas industry distracted it from properly considering security of supply issues.

Was privatisation a cause of the failure of supply?

The above statement stops short of claiming that privatisation was a *cause* of the failure of supply. Since this book is an attempt to identify causal factors, this issue needs to be considered explicitly. It will be recalled that "cause" was given a quite precise meaning in Chapter 2. For a factor to count as a cause it needs to be shown that in the absence of that factor the outcome would have been different. In the present case one needs to be able to argue that in the absence of privatisation, supply would have been more secure. But suppose privatisation had not been on the agenda. Is it not possible that government might have been focused on something else, for instance, a more rapid expansion of the gas distribution network to rural areas, which distracted attention from the issue of security of supply just as much as did the privatisation focus? If so, the causal argument is weakened. If the alternative to privatisation is another set of equally distracting circumstances, one cannot say: but for privatisation, supply would have been more secure.

It follows from this discussion that, in order to be able to claim that privatisation was a cause of the lack of focus on supply, greater attention must be paid to the counter-factual situation, that is, the imagined situation in which privatisation is not on the agenda.

Moreover, it needs to be borne in mind that supply had not been secure in the past. Thus, in order to support a causal argument, the counter-factual situation to be imagined is not simply the status quo at the time privatisation was initiated, but a situation which had evolved since that time in such a way that alternative sources of supply had been developed which would have compensated, at least in part, for the total loss of supply from Longford. In short, the counter-factual situation to be imagined is one in which alternative supplies are available – perhaps from an underground storage at Port Campbell and also a high capacity interconnection with the New South Wales system. It is only if such a scenario can plausibly be imagined that one can conclude that privatisation contributed to the gas crisis.

Privatisation was a central feature of the agenda of the Kennett Liberal government, elected to power in October 1992 and still in power at the time of the Longford accident. One way of imagining the alternative is to suppose that Labor had remained in power throughout this period.

Labor had decided not to privatise the Gas and Fuel Corporation in 1992. But privatisation had been an option actively considered by the then government. Moreover, the Gas and Fuel Corporation had been restructured during 1992 in such as a way as to focus on profit. It had shed 20 per cent of its workforce over two years and had been transformed from a single entity into seven largely autonomous business units (Gas and Fuel Corporation Annual Report 91/92). Clearly, aspects of the privatisation agenda were already in train at the time that Labor lost power, thus undermining the value of the imagined alternative for present purposes.

To overcome this problem one must go a little further back, to a time when these trends had not yet emerged. Suppose that the Gas and Fuel Corporation had continued to operate in the 1990s with the same priorities it displayed in the '80s. Would the projects such as the Port Campbell underground storage have been in operation by 1998?

The annual reports of the Corporation in earlier decades contain frequent references to projects undertaken with the aim of improving security of supply. Consistent with this concern, the Corporation recommended in 1988 that the Port Campbell underground storage project go ahead. Moreover, annual reports in this earlier period noted that one of the Corporation's objectives was "to operate as an efficient business enterprise at a level of profit consistent with its role as a publicly-owned utility". This implied that the Corporation was not just a profit-making enterprise but was also pursuing other objectives, such as security of supply.

If the imagined alternative involves projecting the Corporation as it was in the '80s into the future, and presumes governments willing to allow the Corporation to implement the priorities it had at this time, is it reasonable to suppose that the Port Campbell underground storage facility, or a high capacity interconnection with New South Wales, would have been in operation by 1998?

Unfortunately this imagined alternative is so highly speculative that the question is probably unanswerable. Certainly there is no evidence provided in the opposition's submission which would enable one to answer it. It is important to go through this exercise, however, because it demonstrates that there is no certainty that, but for privatisation, supply would have been significantly more secure by 1998. It shows, in other words, that one cannot claim, with any confidence, that privatisation contributed to the failure of supply.

It is of course possible to make other statements. For instance, it is clear that the policy of privatisation systematically failed to address security of supply. It is probably also true that the privatised regime gave less attention to security of supply than did the regime of the 1980s. What cannot be known is whether this would have made a difference on 25 September 1998.

Chapter

10

Selecting Causes

Preceding chapters have identified a wide array of factors which contributed to the Longford disaster. We have noted, too, that the parties at the Royal Commission highlighted some of these and neglected or denied others. This chapter has three purposes. The first is to lay out as completely as possible, in a diagrammatic form, the conclusions about causation which have emerged. The second is to describe, in a more systematic way, the causes which the parties chose to focus on, and the third is to identify the principles of selection which guided these choices.

There are various diagrammatic ways of laying out causal networks available in the literature (eg; Reason, 1997, chap 1; Maurino et al, 1995:24), but for present purposes the most useful is the AcciMap developed by Rasmussen (1997). Figure 1 (over page) presents such a map or diagram of the causal factors leading to the explosion at Longford and loss of gas supply to Victoria. A number of features of this map will be explained in this chapter.

The accident sequence

Level 1, the bottom level of the diagram, lays out the sequence of events – physical processes and operator actions – which constitute the accident sequence. The two irregular stars represent the critical outcomes – explosion and loss of supply. The circles represent the operator errors which contributed to the accident. The sequence starts with the incorrect operation of the bypass valve which allowed condensate to spill over into other parts of the system eventually causing the failure of the warm oil pumps. This led to a metal heat exchanger becoming super cold and therefore brittle. Operators then made the error of restarting the warm oil flow which caused the heat exchanger to fracture, allowing a large volume of gas to escape and ignite. Two men were killed and eight others injured. Because gas plants 2 and 3 were not effectively isolated from the damaged gas plant 1, gas supply from all three plants at the site ceased. And because there was no alternative supply, Victoria was in chaos for two weeks. (A more complete description of the accident sequence is provided in the appendix.)

Increasing causal remoteness

The vertical axis involves a series of levels, increasingly remote from the accident sequence just described. There is a certain amount of arbitrariness in the division into five discrete levels, but the basic principle is – the more remote the cause, the higher up the diagram it is located. I have numbered the levels from bottom to top because the following discussion works upwards from the bottom.

Level 2 consists of the many organisational factors which have been identified in this book as contributing to the disaster. Thus, for instance, the left side of the panel shows how the absence of engineers on site at Longford cascaded down to cause the incorrect bypass valve operation which started the accident sequence. Because management determines how an organisation operates, these are essentially management system failures. The octagonal box includes the factors singled out by the Royal Commission as the "real causes" of the disaster.

Level 3 is the corporate or company level. It includes matters of company structure and board room financial decisions. It can be seen from the diagram that the drive to cut costs contributed in a pervasive way to the final outcome. Three particular effects were identified in earlier chapters: the decision to remove the engineers from Longford, the reduction in spending on maintenance and the resulting backlog, and the failure to carry out the HAZOP of gas plant 1. It is noteworthy that the Royal Commission was willing to come to a similar conclusion.

Figure 1 - Causal Diagram of Esso Gas Plant Accident

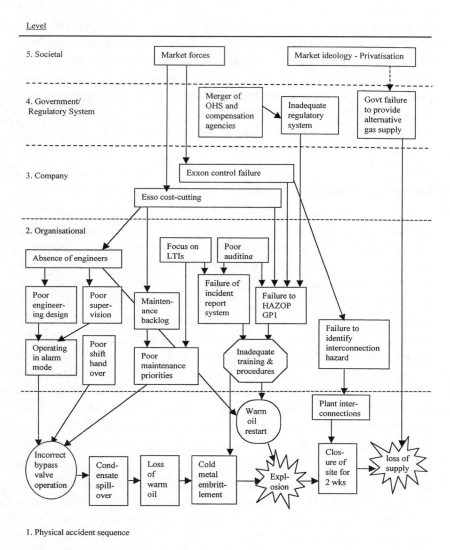

Insofar as the failure to conduct the HAZOP study for GP1 and the reduction of supervision at Longford, including the transfer of engineers to Melbourne, were the result of Esso's desire to control its operating costs, asset management practices or policies may have been a contributing factor to the explosion, fire and failure of gas supply (Dawson, 15.7).

Level 4 covers government and the regulatory system. Level 5, at the top of the diagram, is what I have termed the societal level. We live in an increasingly global, capitalist society in which competition and the market affect most aspects of our lives. The effect is two-fold.

First, market forces drive corporate decision-making in obvious ways. Market forces generated constant cost-cutting efforts by Esso throughout the 1990s, with the consequences described above. It is interesting to note that this was part of a world-wide phenomenon. In the UK, the oil industry formalised its drive to reduce costs in what was called the Cost Reduction in the New Era (CRINE) initiative. CRINE sources asserted that "capital and operating costs have continued to escalate ... [and] unless urgent action is taken to reverse this trend, the future of oil and gas development in the UK North Sea will be in serious jeopardy" (quoted in Whyte, 1997:1151). The threat was from the international market place, in particular, cheaper production costs in Mexico, Vietnam, the Maldives, China, Indonesia and Malaysia. Toombs and Whyte (1998) argue that resources available for safety in the North Sea increased in the aftermath of the Piper Alpha disaster in 1988 but that the cost cutting associated with CRINE saw a reduction in safety-related spending and a consequent impact on safety. It is clear that the impact of market forces on safety at Longford was part of a much broader pattern.

Moreover, as was noted in chapter 3, the cost-cutting imperative drove large corporations in the 1980s to decentralise, which meant that head office handed over responsibility for safety to operating subsidiaries. Consequently, in matters of safety, companies like Esso Australia were not subject to effective control by their parent company.

The second way in which the market affects us is ideologically. Associated with contemporary market society is a *belief* that the market is the best way to satisfy human wants and needs and that governments should play as small a role as possible in this process.

This has led to the prevailing ideologies of privatisation and de-regulation. Chapter 9 considered in detail the hypothesis that privatisation contributed to the gas crisis.

The causal connections

The arrows in Figure 1 are to be understood as meaning cause in the sense that has been used in this book, namely, one thing is said to be a cause of another if we can say: but for the first the second would not have occurred. Note that because one of the causal connections at the top of the diagram could not be plausibly established in this "but for" sense, it is indicated with a dotted line.

Defining cause in this way has various consequences. First, there is a theoretically unlimited number of factors or circumstances giving rise to any particular event; the ones represented here are those which have been discussed in the text. It should be acknowledged, too, that not all the causal factors which came to light in the inquiry have been dealt with in this book. In particular, metallurgical causes have not been dealt with.

Second, the definition implies that had any one of these causal pathways in the diagram been absent the outcome would probably not have occurred. Take for example the box "failure to HAZOP GP1" in level 2. This box has four arrows leading to it. This is to be understood as follows.

- Had high quality auditing been carried out it would have picked up the fact that no HAZOP had been done of GP1 and presumably would have recommended this course of action.

- Had Esso not been so focused on cost cutting it would have carried out the HAZOP and identified the problem which led to the accident.

- Had Exxon exercised greater control over Esso in matters of safety, it would have ensured that Esso HAZOPed GP1 with special attention to cold metal embrittlement.

- Had the regulatory system been based on safety case principles, Esso would have been required to HAZOP GP1.

The four causal pathways leading to this box thus represent four ways in which the accident might have been forestalled.

Of course, each of the four claims above is contestable: we cannot say that had the matters been different in the ways described the HAZOP would *certainly* have been done. We can say, merely, that based on the available evidence it is *likely* that it would have been carried out. Most of the causal statements implied in the diagram need to be understood as qualified in this way.

Initial causal selection by government

The preceding discussion lays out the causal analysis carried out in this book as systematically as possible. None of the participants in the inquiry addressed all of these causal factors. Each chose to focus on particular causes. The rest of this chapter lays out the choices made by the major players and explores the principles of selection they used. Fourteen parties appeared before the Commission and not all will be covered here.

As a background to this discussion we need to note a preliminary principle of causal selection which the State government sought to impose on the Commission. The terms of reference for the Commission, set by the government, were to inquire into and report on the following matters.

1. What were the causes of:

    (a) the explosion and fire ...

    (b) the failure of gas supply from the Longford facilities ...

2. Whether any of the following factors caused or contributed to the occurrence of that explosion, fire and failure of gas supply, namely:

    (a) the design of the Longford facilities including the interdependence of the

        (i) plants ... and

        (ii) the Longford facilities and other facilities at, or upstream of, the Esso site at Longford;

    (b) operating standards, practices and policies;

    (c) maintenance standards, practices and policies;

    (d) asset management practices and policies;

(e)   risk management procedures and emergency procedures ...

(f)   any relevant changes to the above

(g)   the hydrate incident ...

(h)   whether there was any breach of, or non-compliance with, the requirements of any relevant statute or regulation by Esso ...

3.   What steps should be taken by Esso ... to prevent or lessen the risks of

(a)   a repetition of the incident ...

(b)   a further disruption of gas supply from those facilities.

These terms effectively precluded the possibility of the Commission investigating the role of the government in the crisis. Notice in particular that clause 1(b) requires the Commission to consider "the failure of gas supply from the Longford facilities ...", not the failure of supply to consumers. To have investigated the failure of supply to consumers would have raised the question addressed in the previous chapter of why there was no alternative source to compensate for the failure of supply from Longford. This was clearly something the government did not want the Commission to address.

Clause 2(a) allowed the Commission to investigate whether interdependence of the Longford site with facilities upstream, but not downstream of the site, contributed to the accident. Upstream facilities are owned by Esso; facilities immediately downstream are controlled by a government entity, VENCorp. Again, therefore, it appears that the terms seek to prevent the Commission from examining the role of the government.

Finally clause 3 asked the Commission to consider what Esso should do to prevent a recurrence, not what the *government* should do.

The terms of reference therefore amount to a powerful first principle of selection imposed on the Commission by the government, that principle being to avoid any discussion of causes which might implicate the government.

Note that the terms of reference do not specifically invite the Commission to consider whether the regulatory environment contributed to the accident. However the Commission ruled at one point that:

Clause 1 of the terms of reference requires the Commission to inquire into the causes of the explosion and fire and the failure of gas supply and we are of the view that that clause imposes an obligation upon the Commission to inquire whether the regulatory environment ... caused or contributed to those events.

This ruling effectively broadened the inquiry to cover aspects of the regulatory regime which the government had obviously hoped would not be investigated.

The Commissioners

The Royal Commission consisted of two members: a former High Court judge and a technical expert. It was chaired by the judge. Consider now the views on the causes of the disaster expressed in the Commission's report.

Guided by the terms of reference, the Commissioners did not investigate the absence of any alternatives to supply from Longford. In terms of the diagram, their investigation was aimed at explaining the second box from the right on level 1 – "closure of site for two weeks". Their report therefore made no response to the submission by the State opposition discussed in the previous chapter and said nothing about the government's failure to provide an alternative gas supply.

Apart from this, the Commission dealt with most of the other causes identified on the diagram. As noted in Chapter 2, it described the causal connections in level 1 as "immediate" causes. Most of the other connections were described as contributing factors of one sort or another. At one point the Commission noted that it saw no distinction between "a cause" and "a contributing factor". Nevertheless it described "inadequate training and procedures" – the octagonal box – as the "real causes" of the accident. I argued in Chapter 2 that this reflected a legal style of reasoning according to which identifying causes amounts to allocating legal liability – liability to pay damages or liability for punishment. It was, indeed, on the basis of these "real" causes that the Commission found Esso to be liable under the *Victorian Occupational Health and Safety Act* (Dawson, 15.7). Section 21 of the Act provides that:

An employer shall provide and maintain so far as is practicable for employees a working environment that is safe and without risks to health.

The Commission found that:

The failure of Esso to provide a safe working environment in GP1 on 25 September 1998 was the result of its having failed to take measures which were plainly practicable. In order to provide a safe working environment there could and should have been appropriate procedures to deal with the loss of lean oil circulation, cold temperatures and the shutdown and startup of the plant. Furthermore, the operators and supervisors could and should have known of and understood the real hazards confronting them on the day (Dawson, 14.12).

In this passage the Commission is singling out inadequate training and the absence of procedures as the basis for its claim that Esso had violated the OHS Act, that is, as the basis of Esso's liability. It seems likely that this is why it identified these factors as the "real" causes.

At the time of writing, charges have been laid against Esso under the OHS Act. Whether the court in fact finds Esso guilty will depend on the precise detail of what is alleged and on the evidence which Esso is able to present in its defence. Evidence is likely to be produced which was not available to the Royal Commission, so the outcome cannot be predicted. In short, whether the court will agree with the findings of the Royal Commission remains to be seen. The conclusion of the Commission is reported here in order to elucidate the causal thinking of the Commissioners and is not intended to prejudge in any way the outcome of cases pending.

Counsel assisting the Commission

Counsel assisting the Commission directs the research efforts of the Commission staff and, in addition, makes submissions to the Commissioners, in the same way as any other party. Counsel assisting differs from all other counsel, however, in not representing any particular interest. The views of counsel do not necessarily coincide with the views of the Commissioners and are therefore worth discussing separately from those of the Commission.

The submission by counsel assisting addressed what he called "the more pertinent management issues" because, as he noted, "by far the most complex issues facing the Commission are those which concern the contributory role of Esso management systems". He argued, too, that the "attribution of blame by Esso management and experts to the operators exposes Esso to a finding that ... it fail[ed] to implement its extensive and perhaps overwhelming management systems". He concluded as follows.

> *In our submission, Esso's unwillingness to concede relevant deficiencies in its management and management systems following the incident do not engender confidence in its ability to prevent a further disruption to the supply of gas to the State of Victoria. The failure of management to recognise identified shortcomings in the implementation of its ... management system may well have been a factor contributing to the 25 September incident.*

The many causes identified at level 2 of Figure 1 are all matters for which management is responsible. Counsel assisting therefore focused almost exclusively on level 2 causes. Consistent with his approach he had little to say about causal factors at level 4. Also consistent with his approach, though surprising to some, he had nothing to say about the physical causes at level 1.

Esso

As noted in Chapter 2, Esso singled out operator error as the main cause of the accident. Of all the causal factors sketched in Figure 1, its primary focus was on the two circles. It claimed that none of the organisational factors arrayed at level 2 was relevant to the accident. Nor did they constitute evidence that anything was wrong with the way Esso managed safety. The company claimed, in particular, that there was nothing wrong with the training provided to the operators. One of its directors was asked at the Commission:

> *Does Esso continue or intend to continue to conduct its business on the basis that it is satisfied that, as at 25 September 1998, its work management systems were effective?*

The director's answer was a simple – yes.

Esso's position was not simply that operators had made errors but that they alone were responsible for these errors. If it came to questions of legal liability, it was the operators, not Esso, who were to blame.

There was a second causal factor which served Esso's interests – the Victorian Government's failure to provide alternative sources of supply. In this matter Esso was in agreement with the State opposition's position described in Chapter 9. At one point in the inquiry the company sought to introduce evidence to support its argument that the State should take responsibility for security of supply. It claimed that not to accept this evidence would blindfold the Commission and it alleged that Esso was being scapegoated for 30 years of inaction by State governments. The Commission rejected this submission on the basis that the matter lay outside the terms of reference.

BHP

BHP Petroleum was represented at the inquiry because it has a proprietary interest in the Bass Strait project, based on its ownership of the original exploration lease. BHP's role will be touched on again in Chapter 11, but suffice it to say here that BHP takes no part in the actual operation and has no role or responsibility in the management of Longford. BHP's submission as to the causes of the accident was confined to asserting vigorously that, because of its non-operational role, it was in no way responsible for what happened. It chose to make no other submission as to cause, and thus avoided blaming Esso, or for that matter any other party. This choice was no doubt influenced by the fact that it is in ongoing partnership with Esso in Bass Strait and had nothing to gain by criticising its partner.

On-site unions

The on-site unions represented the workers at Longford. The primary aim of their submission was to defend their members against charges of operator error. They noted that Esso "chose to do no more than blame its own workers in an attempt to justify its systems". The proper course, they argued, would be to "attribute blame to Esso". They concluded as follows:

> We submit this Commission ought ... to make findings against
> Esso which are not based on operator error. We submit that

Esso's "negligence" and statutory breaches were the sole cause of the explosion, fire and interruption to gas supply.

Consistent with this position, the submission endorsed the causal network at levels 2 and 3. Causal factors at the level of the government and regulatory system are more remote and nothing much was to be gained in terms of protecting the workers from blame by arguing that factors at this level might have contributed to the explosion. They were therefore not the focus of the submission.

The Insurance Council of Australia

Insurance companies paid out hundreds of millions of dollars to gas customers who had suffered damage as a result of the loss of gas supply. They planned to sue Esso and had a strong interest in encouraging the Commission to find that Esso was negligent. The Insurance Council of Australia was therefore represented at the inquiry and introduced its submission as follows.

The Longford explosion and the failure of gas supply following same were caused by the negligence of Esso Australia Ltd. This Submission is confined to an analysis of the conduct of the company and a particularisation of the areas in which it was negligent.

The submission therefore focused on levels 1, 2 and 3 of the causal diagram.

Victorian Trades Hall Council

The Victorian Trades Hall Council (THC) represented the interests of Victorian workers generally and was concerned that the government's regulatory system was failing to secure their safety. It believed that self-regulation had amounted to deregulation, in part because WorkCover was not devoting sufficient resources to the enforcement of the law. It is worth noting, in passing, that in the wake of Longford and the continuing campaign by the THC, WorkCover eventually agreed to devote more resources to inspection and prosecution (*The Age*, 3/8/99).

For the THC, then, the burning issue was whether or not the regulatory system had contributed to the disaster. Part way through the inquiry, the secretary of the THC expressed the following view:

The Longford Royal Commission has so far concentrated on the nuts-and-bolts details of the gas tragedy. But while Esso is - and should be – at the centre of the inquiry, responsibility for safety and security of our gas supply is not the company's alone. The inquiry should be broadened to include examination of regulations, legislation and actions of the State government (The Age, 21/1/99).

Counsel for the THC put this to the Commission which ruled, as noted above, that the Commission already had the power to inquire into the regulatory environment. The way was now open for the THC to argue in its final submission that there were deficiencies in the regulatory system which needed to be remedied by the adoption of a safety case regime. Consistent with this argument, its principal submission as to cause was that "deficiencies in the existing regulatory regime caused or contributed to the fire". The THC argued that causal analysis in the context of the Royal Commission was an exercise aimed at fact finding, not the determination of liability, and that its claim about causation was not intended as a claim about legal liability.

In terms of the diagram, the submission by the THC gave major emphasis to level 4. But it also dealt with most of the causal factors laid out in levels 1 to 3.

The State opposition

The State opposition was represented at the inquiry because, as it said, it had a "special interest in ascertaining whether there was a failure in the processes of governance". The Kennett Liberal government had been pursuing a vigorous policy of privatisation of urban services such as electricity and gas distribution, in conjunction with a policy of what it called a "light-handed" approach to regulation. The opposition regarded this agenda of privatisation and deregulation as detrimental to the citizens of Victoria in numerous ways, and its submission sought to show, in particular, that these policies had contributed to the gas crisis. Its submissions as to cause, therefore, were that "legislative deficiencies contributed to the disaster" and that "the current culture of privatisation and deregulation contributed to the disaster". The opposition also argued that the Victorian WorkCover Authority had "failed to properly inspect and regulate the Esso Longford site and ...

that the government's move to self-regulation has contributed to a deterioration in VWA's practices". Finally the opposition's submission noted that "Esso failed in its responsibility to ensure a safe workplace", but it said nothing about the organisational causes of the problem. Consistent with its purposes, then, the opposition's causal analysis focused almost exclusively on levels 4 and 5 of Figure 1.

The State government

Although the State government had set the terms of reference, the way the Commission had interpreted them made it necessary for the State to defend itself in its final submission. It urged the Commission to find that Esso was *solely* responsible for the accident, and that no other party was in any way implicated. In particular, the government was not to blame – neither WorkCover, self-regulation nor the privatisation of the gas system could be said to have contributed in any way to the problem. "The existing regulatory environment and the action or inaction of any government agency did not cause or contribute to the Longford incident". Given this position it is not surprising that the submission endorsed most of the causes identified in levels 2 and 3 of the diagram, but denied the causal impact of level 4 and said nothing about level 5.

The submission did however go on to support the view that a safety case regime was necessary to deal with facilities like Longford, thereby implicitly admitting that the existing regulatory environment was inadequate. It made the point that no regulatory environment could guarantee safety and therefore it could not be said with certainty that a safety case regime would have averted the accident. But it follows from the State's argument that had a safety case regime been in place the accident at Longford would have been less likely to occur. Given the definition of cause used here, the implication is that the inadequacy of the regulatory regime was a possible or perhaps even probable cause of the accident. The fact that the State was so keen to avoid any such conclusion must be understood as motivated by the desire to avoid any legal liability or even criticism for what happened.

Victorian WorkCover

The submission of the Victorian WorkCover Authority was largely aimed at forestalling any criticism of the Authority. It argued not only that all allegations against WorkCover itself were unfounded but that there was "no basis upon which it can be responsibly asserted that the regulatory scheme in force at the time contributed to the incident". This is the same claim made in the submission by the State government, for the same self-defensive reason, and its problematic character has already been noted.

WorkCover submitted that the explosion "was solely produced by the acts and omissions of Esso ... [and] responsibility for the incident rests squarely with the failure by Esso to identify and control hazards ...". Consistent with this position, WorkCover subsequently announced its intention to prosecute Esso. Predictably, WorkCover endorsed the causal network up to and including level three, but not higher levels.

Principles of selection

Chapter 2 introduced the idea of a network or chain of causation. Based on the analysis carried out in this book the present chapter has identified this network of causes and arranged them in five levels: physical, organisational, company, govermental/regulatory and societal, in increasing order of causal remoteness.

Chapter 2 also introduced the concept of stop rule – the idea that parties will move back along the causal pathways to different points, determined by the implicit stop rules with which they are operating. This is an invaluable idea. However the stop rule concept needs to be understood in a particular way in the present context. The parties at the Longford inquiry did not necessarily acknowledge all the causal factors back to the point at which they stopped. Indeed some of them skipped back along the causal chain, acknowledging some and ignoring or denying others. Thus, Esso selected causes at levels 1 and 4 but denied the causal relevance of factors at levels 2 and 3. Again, the State opposition focused exclusively on level 4 and said nothing in its submission about lower levels.

For this reason I have chosen in the present chapter to talk of principles of selection, or selection rules, rather than stop rules. Three principles can be seen in operation in the submissions examined. These are outlined below.

First, where parties had financial or reputational interests at stake, this guided their selection of cause above all else. In particular, those seeking to avoid blame or criticism focused resolutely on factors which assigned blame elsewhere, and denied, sometimes in the face of overwhelming evidence, the causal significance of factors which might have reflected adversely on them. Esso and the on-site unions were guided by this principle of emphasising causes which diverted blame elsewhere. The Insurance Council of Australia was likewise guided by financial interest in identifying negligence by Esso as the cause of the accident. It is obvious that parties with direct interests will be guided by these interests in their selection of causes. Only where the participants have agendas not based on immediate self-interest, can other principles of causal selection come into play.

A second principle emerges for participants whose primary concern is accident prevention. It is to focus on causes which are controllable, from the participants' point of view. It can be argued that the Trades Hall Council, the State opposition and counsel assisting the Commission all selected causes on this basis.

Consider the Trades Hall Council's position. It had no direct influence over Esso and therefore no capacity to bring about the kinds of management changes in Esso which might prevent a recurrence. However, it did have the potential to influence government and government agencies. Its strategy, therefore, was to seek changes in the regulatory system which would compel Esso and similar companies to improve their management of safety. This is the point in the causal network where intervention by the THC was likely to be most effective. Hence its emphasis on the regulatory system as the cause of the accident.

Consider, next, the State opposition. Sceptics will no doubt see the opposition's submission as a politically motivated attack on the government. But there is more to it than this. The opposition was convinced that privatisation had been detrimental to Victorians in a number of ways and that the privatisation of the gas distribution system was a case in point. Moreover, the opposition was the alternative government, and when next in power it would be in a position to do something about the privatisation of gas distribution, if it were plausibly established that this had contributed to the problem. This was a matter far more amenable to government decision-making than was Esso's management system, for example. It made sense, therefore, for the opposition to focus at this point in the network of causation.

Counsel assisting was another participant with no particular interest to defend who gravitated towards an accident prevention perspective. He, of course, had no special access to government and therefore no reason to dwell on causes at this level. In any case, intervention at more remote points in the causal network is aimed at bringing about changes in company management systems. Safety experts almost universally regard management systems as the key to the prevention of accidents and, conversely, failures of management as the key to understanding accidents. The Commission's research director was such an expert and he no doubt contributed to the decision by counsel assisting to focus on Esso's management system failures as the critical causal factors.

In all three cases, then, selection of cause was driven by judgments about where in the causal network intervention might be most effective, from an accident prevention point of view. The THC and State opposition both believed they had some capacity to influence causes at the government/regulatory level, and selected causes accordingly. Counsel assisting focused on factors under management control, for reasons given above.

WorkCover and the State government were motivated to adopt both principles discussed above. On the one hand, the principle of avoiding blame led them to assert that the regulatory system was in no way a cause of the accident. On the other hand, they were concerned about accident prevention, and their regulatory role led them both to propose an alternative, safety case regime. This was an implicit admission that the existing system had contributed to the accident in the "but for" sense. The strained nature of their submissions in this respect was a direct result of the simultaneous operation of these two principles of selection.

The Royal Commission adopted a third principle of selection, namely to focus on causes which generate legal liability. As explained above, the factors it chose to identify as real causes were the very factors which led it to conclude that Esso had breached the Victorian *Occupational Health Safety Act.*

Three distinct principles of causal selection, based on three different perspectives, have now been identified as being in operation at the Commission.

- Self-interest: select causes consistent with self-interest.

- Accident prevention: select causes which are most controllable.

- The legal perspective: select causes which generate legal liability.

For certain parties, more than one of these principles was at work. The cases of WorkCover and the State government have been mentioned. Another example is the Insurance Council, for which the principle of self-interest coincided with the principle of selecting causes which generated legal liability.

Two causal factors were demonstrated in this book to have played an important role – market forces and Exxon's hands-off approach – yet neither was selected for emphasis by any of the participants. This is worth elaborating.

Exxon was not a party to the proceedings, nor was its contribution to the accident investigated, presumably because it was not mentioned in the terms of reference. Nevertheless, Exxon cast a shadow over the whole inquiry. Its personnel carried out Esso's initial accident investigation which highlighted the fact that GP1 had not been subjected to a HAZOP study, but they then departed the country and remained effectively out of reach of the Commission. Enough information emerged at the inquiry, however, to be able to draw certain conclusions about Exxon's role (see Chapter 3).

The other factor ignored by all parties (despite the fact that, in an important sense, it was the ultimate cause of the disaster) was the market. There are obvious reasons for this blind spot. Capitalist society is a given – the taken-for-granted context of the world of work. There is no realistic prospect of cutting ourselves off from global market society in the interests of accident prevention. Moreover, many would argue that, for other reasons, such a course of action is not even desirable. There was therefore nothing to be gained for any participant by drawing attention to this ultimate cause.

It can now be suggested that the reason these two factors were passed over by participants is that none of the principles discussed above led to their selection. Specifically, no party had a direct interest in highlighting them; they are not readily controllable; and they do not give rise to legal liability. Clearly, the principles of selection are necessarily also principles of exclusion. Understanding how they operate provides considerable insight into the causal arguments produced at the Royal Commission.

Chapter

11

An Absence of Mindfulness

The causal analysis in this book has been carried out at several levels. Nevertheless, most of the contributing factors identified were organisational failures, for which Esso's management is ultimately responsible. Given the number of such factors, there is clearly a need for some kind of conceptual clarification. Is there some overarching concept which will serve to summarise and at the same time bring coherence to this array of organisational failures? In this final chapter I want to explore the concept of organisational mindfulness, developed by theorists of high reliability, and to argue that Esso's failures amount to an absence of mindfulness.

The mindfulness of high reliability organisations

The theory of high reliability organisations was developed in reaction to Perrow's so-called normal accident theory. After studying the 1979 Three Mile Island nuclear accident, Perrow concluded that accidents were inevitable in such high risk, high tech environments. Other researchers disagreed. They noted that there were numerous examples of high risk, high tech organisations which functioned with extraordinary reliability – high reliability organisations (HROs) – and they set about studying what it was that accounted for this reliability. Weick and his colleagues summarise the findings from these studies in a word – mindfulness.

Typical HROs – modern nuclear power plants, naval aircraft carriers, air traffic control systems – operate in an environment where it is not possible to adopt the strategy of learning from mistakes. Since disasters are rare in any one organisation the opportunities for making improvements based on one's own experience are too limited to be made use of in this way. Moreover, even one disaster is one too many. Management must find ways of avoiding disaster altogether. The strategy which HROs adopt is collective mindfulness. The essence of this idea is that no system can guarantee safety once and for all. Rather, it is necessary for the organisation to cultivate a state of continuous mindfulness of the possibility of disaster. "Worries about failure are what give HROs much of their distinctive quality." HROs exhibit a "prideful wariness" and a "suspicion of quiet periods". (These and following quotes are from Weick, 1999:92-7.)

HROs seek out localised small-scale failures and generalise from them. "They act as if there is no such thing as a localised failure and suspect instead that causal chains that produced the failure are long and wind deep inside the system."

"Mindfulness involves interpretative work directed at weak signals." Incident-reporting systems are therefore highly developed and people rewarded for reporting. Weick et al cite the case of "a seaman on the nuclear carrier Carl Vinson who loses a tool on the deck, reports it, all aircraft aloft are redirected to land bases until the tool is found and the seaman is commended for his actions the next day at a formal deck ceremony".

One consequence of this approach is that "maintenance departments in HROs become central locations for organisational learning". Maintenance workers are the front line observers, in a position to give early warning of ways in which things might be going wrong.

The preoccupation of HROs with failure means that they are willing to countenance redundancy – the deployment of more people than is necessary in the normal course of events so that there are enough people on hand to deal with abnormal situations when they arise. This availability of extra personnel ensures operators are not placed in situations of overload which may threaten their performance. A mindful organisation exhibits "extraordinary sensitivity to the incipient overloading of any one of its members", as when air traffic controllers gather around a colleague to watch for danger during times of peak air traffic.

If HROs are pre-occupied with failure, more conventional organisations focus on their success. They interpret the absence of disaster as evidence of their competence and of the skillfulness of their managers. The focus on success breeds confidence that all is well. "Under the assumption that success demonstrates competence, people drift into complacency, inattention, and habitual routines." They use their success to justify the elimination of what is seen as unnecessary effort and redundancy. The result for such organisations is that "current success makes future success less probable".

Esso's lack of mindfulness

It must already be apparent from this discussion that Esso did not exhibit the characteristics of a mindful organisation. In this section I shall summarise the organisational failures which led to the accident and show how they amounted to an absence of mindfulness. Discussion will proceed from left to right on level 2 of Figure 1 in Chapter 10.

The withdrawal of engineers from the Longford site in 1992 was very clearly a retreat from mindfulness. The presence of engineers was a form of redundancy which meant that trouble-shooting expertise was always on hand. Operators could rely on them for a second and expert opinion and their expertise enabled them to know when the quick fix or the easy solution was inappropriate and a more thoroughgoing response might be necessary. It was the absence of the engineers on site which enabled the practice of operating the plant in alarm mode to develop unchecked and without any consideration being given to the possible dangers involved. The huge number of alarms which operators were expected to cope with meant that they worked at times in situations of quite impossible overload, something which would not have been permitted by any organisation mindful of what can go wrong under such circumstances. The withdrawal of engineers also meant that there was no trouble-shooting expertise available on the day of the accident.

Communication failure between shifts is another aspect of Esso's lack of mindfulness. Operators who had been encouraged to be alert to how things might go wrong would naturally interrogate the previous shift for information about problems which might occur on their own shift.

There was no such awareness or process at Longford, where the absence of failure had bred an assumption that successful operation could be expected.

A further matter noted above was the critical nature of maintenance activity as an opportunity for organisational learning. This was not how maintenance was viewed at Esso. Maintenance staff were "cut till it hurt" and the result was a maintenance backlog. Maintenance was then prioritised in a way which did not pay attention to the possibility that breakdowns might have causal chains or perhaps chains of consequence that "are long and wind deep inside the system". The failure to repair the TRC3B valve had just such consequences.

An active and effective incident reporting system is the hallmark of a mindful organisation. Esso's reporting system was quite inadequate in this respect. It was used to report lost-time injuries, but process upsets were not reported, unless they affected production. In so doing Esso failed to avail itself of the opportunity to investigate matters which might provide warning of catastrophic failure. The outstanding example of this was the failure to record and then investigate the cold temperature incident which occurred a month before the accident. Such an investigation would have identified the inadequate training and procedures which led to the disastrous decision by operators and their supervisors to restart the warm oil system.

Organisations mindful of the possibility of failure would take every opportunity to identify hazards. Esso's failure to carry out the HAZOP of GP1 was thus a failure of mindfulness. So, too, were the company's various failures to conduct the risk assessments of change which its own guidelines required it to do and the failure to carefully assess the hazards of interconnectedness.

On top of all of this, safety auditing, an ideal opportunity to focus on the possibility of failure, was turned into an opportunity to celebrate success.

Learning the lessons from elsewhere

Mindfulness about the possibility of failure extends to learning the lessons from elsewhere. Esso did not have to look very far afield for relevant lessons, but seemed to lack the capacity or motivation to do so.

Lessons from Exxon

There were, for instance, lessons from the parent company, Exxon, which Esso failed to learn. Instances of brittle fracture had occurred in other Exxon plants and had led Exxon to express particular concern about this problem. But Esso had not acted on this information in relation to gas plant 1.

Lessons from Piper Alpha

The Piper Alpha fire also offered lessons which Esso failed to learn. One such lesson was the need to be able to isolate plant or production units so that a fire at one could not be fed by oil or gas from another. Related to this was the need to ensure that the failure of one plant did not impede production from others. Had this lesson been learnt and acted on the impact of the fire in gas plant 1 on Victoria's gas supply would have been far less.

Another lesson from Piper Alpha was that high quality auditing should be conveying at least some bad news to the top of the organisation. "Continuous good news – you worry", was the message which had been broadcast to the industry. Yet the Exxon audit of Esso some months before the explosion conveyed only good news to Esso's board.

Ironically, there was an earlier incident which should have alerted Esso to the importance of learning from Piper Alpha. Some ten months after Piper Alpha, Esso had a fire on its Tuna platform in Bass Strait. The Victorian Coroner who investigated the Tuna fire was so struck by what he called the "remarkable similarities in the respective causes" of the two fires that he devoted part of his report to demonstrating these similarities (Johnstone, 1991:8-12). Both fires resulted from a lack of coordination between shifts and, in particular: "inadequately developed and followed work permits, danger tagging and lockout procedures". Moreover, in both cases the fire extinguishing system had been allowed to fall into partial disrepair and did not work properly. Information about these failures on Piper Alpha was available to Esso prior to the Tuna fire but the problems had not been rectified, allowing an almost carbon copy event to occur.

The coroner observed, further, that in the nine years prior to his report there had been no fewer than twenty fires reported on Bass Strait platforms – at least one of these, in 1986, involving a fatality. He went on:

> *a history of fires and incidents in Bass Strait and overseas (including Piper Alpha) clearly indicates the obvious risk where even the smallest error can lead to a potential for disaster. The lessons ought to have been learnt well before 1989.*

The coroner was especially critical of Esso's auditing.

> *Effective audit of the deluge system and fire fighting equipment on Tuna ought to have identified and rectified the problems associated with items such as blocked fire hose nozzles well before the fire ... Effective audit also ought to have identified the shortcomings in the permit, danger tagging and lockout procedures which would have prevented the* [Tuna] *event.*

Clearly, given the lessons of Piper Alpha and Esso's own earlier experience in Bass Strait, there was no shortage of lessons about the importance of auditing for Esso to draw on at Longford.

Lessons from Moura

Finally, there were the lessons from the Moura mine disaster, directly applicable to Longford, about communication failure, incident reporting, the need to focus on catastrophic risks and yet again, the failure of auditing. BHP Coal had learnt these lessons and its corporate audit of 1996 was a model of mindful auditing – attuned to the possibilities of failure and conveying bad news to the top of the hierarchy.

It might be objected at this point that coal mining is a different industry and that there is no reason to expect even a mindful company to be attentive to lessons in other industries. But consider the following two facts.

First, Esso has a particular interest in the coal industry. In 1998 Esso Australia Resources was 100 per cent owner of one New South Wales coal mine and Exxon Coal Australia owned 36 per cent of another. At the highest corporate level, then, Exxon/Esso had a direct interest in the coal industry and therefore an interest in whatever lessons there were to be learnt from Moura.

Second, Moura mine was operated by BHP Coal, which is owned, ultimately, by BHP Ltd, the company listed on the stock exchange.

BHP Ltd also owns BHP Petroleum (BHPP), which is a half owner of the Bass Strait project, receiving half the benefits and sharing equally with Esso in the costs of the joint undertaking. BHPP takes no part in the actual operation which is entirely Esso's responsibility. Nevertheless, it is represented on a supervisory committee which approves capital expenditure budgets submitted by Esso as operator. The result is that BHPP has a unique opportunity for vigilance in relation to safety, via the budget process. Here then is a second reason why the experience at Moura was directly relevant to Longford: Moura's ultimate owner was the ultimate owner of 50 per cent of the Bass Strait operation and thus in a special position to pass on the lessons of Moura to Esso.

It seems, however, that although BHP and Esso/Exxon had interests in both industries, this did not facilitate the transfer of learning from one industry to the other. The policy of decentralising responsibility for safety to the operating level, which was followed by both Esso/Exxon and BHP, meant that at the top of the corporate structure, where the linkages between the petroleum and coal industries existed, there was little capacity for ensuring that lessons leant by operating companies in one industry were passed on to operating companies in another (see further, Hopkins, 1999, chap 9). The corporate structures of both BHP and Esso/Exxon militated against mindfulness in this respect.

Explaining the absence of mindfulness

Earlier in this chapter, mindfulness was described as an overarching or organising concept, designed to bring coherence to an array of findings. It identifies the principal characteristic of high reliability organisations, but it does not explain why they are the way they are. Describing Esso's various organisational failures as a failure to be mindful is not, therefore, an *explanation* for these failures.

Why are some organisations mindful and others not? To answer this question, consider for a moment the kinds of organisations which have been identified as high reliability organisations. Nuclear aircraft carriers and air traffic control authorities are not profit-making operations. They are not judged by their stakeholders in terms of economic efficiency or return on investment. Their primary goal is reliable or safe operation. In the case of the aircraft carrier, diverting all aircraft aloft to land bases until a tool on deck is found must have been very costly, but cost over-runs can be met by curtailing operations in a way which does not impact on the primary organisational goal. Moreover, there is always the possibility of increased government appropriation. In contrast, cost over-runs in commercial organisations necessarily impact on the primary goal of the organisation – profit.

Nuclear power stations in the US *are* commercial organisations but the experience of Three Mile Island startled the industry into recognising that another such event occurring at any one power station could mean the end of the whole industry. The industry responded collectively by demanding high reliability from its members. What's more, the industry body was able to enforce its demand. In 1988 it secured the sacking of the CEO of one organisation member which was not performing satisfactorily (Rees, 1994:116). There is evidence, however, that commercial pressures are again asserting themselves. Diablo Canyon was one nuclear power station which, in the 1980s, achieved high reliability by employing large numbers of engineering staff to work with its blue collar employees. In the early 1990s, in the face of skyrocketing costs, it cut its staff by half (Bourrier, 1998:144). The impact on reliability is yet to be studied.

The point is that there are particular conditions which facilitate high reliability functioning. These do not apply for most commercial organisations, and in their absence, the drive to enhance economic efficiency becomes the enemy of mindfulness.

The evidence is that this is the explanation for Esso's failure to be mindful. Cost-cutting pressures led Esso to remove its engineering staff from Longford, cost-cutting pressures led it to postpone indefinitely the crucial HAZOP of gas plant 1 and cost-cutting pressures led to the maintenance cutbacks which contributed to the accident. Moreover, this concern about costs had been effectively communicated to the workforce, to the extent that an operator was able to tell the inquiry:

> *I would go so far as to say I faced a dilemma on the day, standing 20 metres from the explosion and the fire, as to whether or not I should activate ESD 1 (Emergency Shutdown 1), because I was, for some strange reason, worried about the possible impact on production.*

Mandating mindfulness?

Given the forces operating in most organisational contexts against mindfulness, the question arises as to whether governments can provide the countervailing pressures to create it. Critics suggest that requiring companies to adopt state-of-the-art safety management systems is not the answer because this encourages the mechanistic belief that safety is assured once you have set up the system (*Weekend Australian*, 3/7/99). They note that setting up a system does not guarantee the continual mindfulness which is the key to reliable operation.

It is true that safety management systems can degenerate into nothing more than complex systems of paper. But they can be prodded into life by vigorous action by regulators, insisting on active employee participation and carrying out searching audits of elements of the system which require ongoing activity, such as incident-reporting systems and management of change requirements. Mandating mindfulness means ensuring that organisations are actively involved in scanning their own activities for signs of trouble and scanning their external environment for lessons which they can apply to themselves. Understanding that the problem is one of mindfulness does not undermine the safety systems approach; it strengthens it, by highlighting the aspects of safety management which need to be stressed if organisations are to achieve high reliability. Moreover, there is no other way. Urging companies to adopt the mindful ways of high reliability organisations is not likely to be effective for organisations subject to constant market pressures to cut costs.

Mindfulness, then, is a useful umbrella concept. It not only organises the findings, but sensitises us to their essence. Furthermore, it provides a criterion for judging a company's safety system – does the system promote the collective mindfulness of danger?

The lessons of Longford

For companies seeking to be mindful, the lessons which emerge from this analysis are as follows.

- Operator error is not an adequate explanation for major accidents.
- Systematic hazard identification is vital for accident prevention.

- Corporate headquarters should maintain safety departments which can exercise effective control over the management of major hazards.

- All major changes, both organisational and technical, must be subject to careful risk assessment.

- Alarm systems must be carefully designed so that warnings of trouble do not get dismissed as normal (normalised).

- Front-line operators must be provided with appropriate supervision and backup from technical experts.

- Routine reporting systems must highlight safety-critical information.

- Communication between shifts must highlight safety-critical information.

- Incident-reporting systems must specify relevant warning signs. They should provide feedback to reporters and an opportunity for reporters to comment on feedback.

- Reliance on lost-time injury data in major hazard industries is itself a major hazard.

- A focus on safety culture can distract attention from the management of major hazards.

- Maintenance cutbacks foreshadow trouble.

- Auditing must be good enough to identify the bad news and to ensure that it gets to the top.

- Companies should apply the lessons of other disasters.

For governments seeking to encourage mindfulness:

- A safety case regime should apply to all major hazard facilities.

Despite the technological complexities of the Longford site, the accident was not inevitable. The principles listed above are hardly novel – they emerge time and again in disaster studies. As the Commission said, measures to prevent the accident were "plainly practicable".

A corrective conclusion

This book has treated the loss of gas supply to Melbourne residents as in some respects the most significant outcome of the explosion and fire. Certainly, it was the loss of supply which led the government to take the extraordinary step of appointing a Royal Commission. Without the economic and political fallout generated by the interruption of gas supply, we would not have seen such an exhaustive investigation and the lessons for disaster prevention would not have emerged so clearly.

In human terms, however, the most tragic outcome of the explosion and fire was the death of two men and the horrendous burns suffered by several others. The economic hardship suffered by other Victorians is potentially compensable, but nothing can compensate the bereaved and the burnt for their suffering. This is the ultimate reason why disasters must be prevented.

To bring back this human dimension, I close with the thoughts of the operator whose words began this book.

> [I am thankful that I escaped the fate of several others, thrown] *through the air like rag dolls. I'm glad ... because my bones weren't shattered, my skin scalded by freezing cold liquid and then flames so hot they cooked flesh to the bone ...*
>
> *Yeah, I'm lucky. Very, very lucky. My wife and children didn't have to endure the torture of eulogies, of burials, of unsaid goodbyes. I'm lucky because they didn't have to wonder if I was going to live through the night. They didn't have to see me comatose, only to awake to a new world of pain and scarring, both physical and mental ...*
>
> *While I'm not facing a lifetime of corrective surgery to mitigate disfigurement, I can't work in a place where I once thought I would spend the next 27 years of my life. I cannot doff my hardhat to a company that blamed me for the deaths of two of my workmates, the burning of five others, the destruction of half a billion dollars of gas plant, and wish them well. I cannot respect a company that would gladly have me face the tearful, bewildered stare of a workmate's bereaved family, while the directors of that company seek refuge in the judicial cocoon of their legal advice.*

Lessons from Longford

So now I ponder ... While Esso sucks gas out of the strait and into their balance sheet at the rate of a million dollars a day. While their lawyers plot and plan. While the burned and injured heal. While the bereaved go on grieving. While my future ebbs and flows on the tidal whim of a corporate sea (*The Age*, 30/9/99).

Appendix

The Normal Process and the Accident Sequence

This appendix provides a more coherent description of the normal process and the accident sequence than is provided in the text. It is nevertheless a simplified version designed for non-technical readers. Those wanting more detail are referred to the report of the Royal Commission.

The normal process

The Longford complex consists of three gas plants and a crude stabilisation plant. These four plants are interconnected, as the processing of gas produces some liquids which are then further processed in the crude stabilisation plant. Similarly, the processing of crude oil in the stabilisation plant produces some gas which is then fed to the gas plants for final processing before sale.

The gas coming ashore from the Bass Strait platforms contains significant amounts of hydrocarbon liquids (condensate) and water. In order to meet the specified quality for sales gas, it is necessary to process the gas to remove all the water and most of the liquifiable components (LPG), and also to remove hydrogen sulphide, a noxious gas present in very small quantities.

The liquids arriving at Longford in the gas stream are removed in a system of large pipes called slugcatchers and all traces of water and hydrogen sulphide are then removed by so-called molecular sieves which preferentially extract these compounds from the gas stream. The LPG components then have to be removed.

Gas plant 1 uses a refrigerated lean oil absorption process for this purpose, so-called because lean oil (a light oil similar to aviation kerosene) is circulated at low temperature over trays in a tower, called an absorber, to extract the LPG components from the gas stream which is passing up the tower. The lean oil is enriched by the LPG which it extracts and is then called rich oil. The processed gas from the top of the tower is piped away for sale and the cold, rich oil leaves the absorber and is heated by passing through several heat exchangers before being distilled to recover the LPG as a marketable product. Having had the LPG components stripped from it, the rich oil becomes lean oil and is circulated back through the system of heat exchangers to return to the absorber as cold, lean oil.

Because the gas entering the absorber is refrigerated, some of the LPG components in it are condensed and this condensate is removed from the gas stream in a separate compartment on the bottom of the absorber before the gas passes up into the main part of the absorber.

The accident sequence

The night before the accident there had been a larger than usual flow of liquids into the plant from offshore. The result was a build-up of the level of condensate in the absorber. The volume of condensate could be controlled to some extent by raising its temperature. However an automatic valve which controlled the temperature, known as TRC3B, was not working properly and operators were using a manual by-pass valve. For reasons discussed in the text, they did not keep the temperature high enough and the build up of condensate continued. The outflow through the condensate outlet was too great for the downstream reprocessing so the outflow rate was automatically reduced. The level of condensate in the absorber tower then rose so high that it went off scale, that is, beyond the point where operators could monitor it. In fact it rose to the point where it overflowed into the rich oil stream.

The presence of condensate in the rich oil stream caused the rich oil to become much colder than normal. This caused an upset in processing equipment downstream which in turn led to an automatic shutdown of pumps which maintained the lean oil flow.

Operators were unable to restart these pumps and they remained shutdown for hours.

Because the circulation of warm lean oil had stopped, two of the heat exchangers became abnormally cold and a thick layer of frost formed on their exterior pipework. The temperature dropped below the design limit and the metal in one exchanger contracted to the point that it began to leak oil onto the ground. Unsuccessful attempts were made to fix this leak by tightening certain bolts. Operators decided to stop the flow into GP1 at this point to try to deal with the situation. This stopped any further flow of cold condensate within the plant. But operators did not depressurise the plant. Rather, they decided to try again to restart the pumps to rewarm the heat exchanger. This was a critical error. The metal in the vessel by this time was so cold that it was brittle and it needed time to thaw out before being rewarmed. Operators succeeded in restarting the pumps and the reintroduction of warm liquid caused fracturing and catastrophic failure of one of the heat exchangers. A large quantity of volatile liquid and gas escaped and was ignited by a nearby ignition source.

(The absorber is illustrated is figure 2.5 of the Royal Commission Report and the heat exchanger, in figure 6.1.)

Figure 6.1 – Schematic view of the GP905 Reboiler

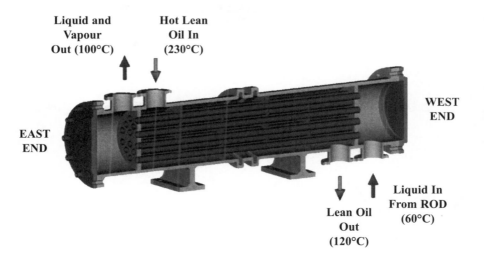

Figure 2.5 – Schematic diagram of an absorber

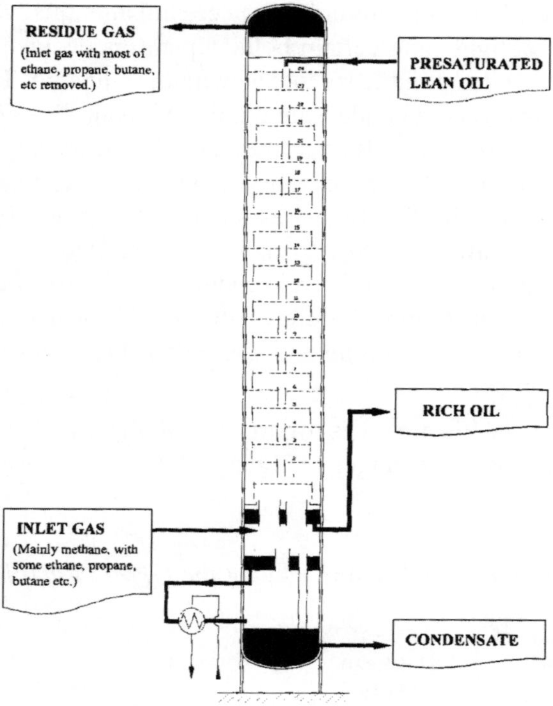

(Diagrams reproduced with permission from the Victorian Government from the Report of the Longford Royal Commission.)

References

ACIL. (1998). *Capturing Near Misses: A Report to BHP Coal.*

Appleton, B. (1994). Piper Alpha. In T. Kletz (Ed.), *Lessons from Disaster: How Organisations Have No Memory and Accidents Recur.* (pp. 174-184). London: Institute of Chemical Engineers.

Bahr, N. (1997). *System Safety Engineering and Risk Assessment: A Practical Approach.* London: Taylor & Francis.

Baram, M. (1997). Shame, blame and liability: Why safety management suffers organisational learning disabilities. In A. Hale, B. Wilpert, & M. Freitag (Ed.), *After the Event: From Accident to Organisational Learning* (pp. 163-177). Oxford: Pergamon.

Baram, M. (1998). Process safety management and the implications of organisational change. In A. Hale, & M. Baram (Ed.), *Safety Management: The Challenge of Change* (pp. 191-206). Oxford: Pergamon.

Barrell, T. (1992). Control of major hazards offshore – implementing Lord Cullen's recommendations. In Institution of Chemical Engineers (Ed.), *Major Hazards Onshore and Offshore* Basingstoke: Taylor & Francis.

BASI (Bureau of Air Safety Investigation). (1995). CAIR Reports. *Air Safety*, (8), 27-32.

Berger, Y. (1999a). Spot the hazard. *Say Safety: The AWU National OHS Magazine*, (September), 40.

Berger, Y. (1999b). Why hasn't it changed on the shopfloor? In C. Mayhew, & C. Peterson (Ed.), *Occupational Health and Safety in Australia* (pp. 52-64). Sydney: Allen & Unwin.

Bourrier, M. (1998). Elements for designing a self-correcting organisation: examples from nuclear plants. In A. Hale & M. Baram (Ed.), *Safety Management: The Challenge of Change* (pp. 133-146). Oxford: Pergamon.

Braithwaite, J. (1985). *To Punish or Persuade: Enforcement of Coal Mine Safety*. Albany: State University of New York.

Braithwaite, J. (1989). *Crime, Shame and Reintegration*. Melbourne: Cambridge University Press.

Brooks, A. (1988). *Guidebook to Australian Occupational Health and Safety Laws. 3rd Edition*. Sydney: CCH Australia.

Carson, W. (1982). *The Other Price of Britain's Oil*. Oxford: Martin Robertson.

Collins, G. (1999). Opening new corridors for Victorian gas. *PESA News* (April, Victorian Supplement), 4.

Cullen, L. (1990). *The Public Inquiry into the Piper Alpha Disaster*. London: HMSO.

Dawson, D. & Brooks, B. (1999). *Report of the Longford Royal Commission: The Esso Longford Gas Plant Accident*. Melbourne: Government Printer for the State of Victoria.

DISR (Department of Industry Science and Resources). (1999). Offshore petroleum safety review issues paper.

DPIE (Department of Primary Industry and Energy). (1995). *Guidelines for Preparation and Submission of Safety Cases*. Canberra: AGPS.

Emmett, E. (1996). Prevention of major accidents in Australia. *Journal of Occupational Health and Safety – ANZ*, 12(5), 581-589.

Emmett, E. A. (1992). New directions for occupational health and safety in Australia. *Journal of Occupational Health and Safety – Australia and New Zealand*, 8(4), 293-308.

Freckelton. (1997). Causation in coronial law. *Journal of Law and Medicine*, 4 (February), 289-298.

Glasbeek, H. & Tucker, E. (1993). Death by consensus: The Westray mine story. *New Solutions*, (Summer), 14-40.

Glen, H. (1993). Business responses to the regulation of health and safety in England. *Law and Policy*, 15 (3 July), 219-233.

Gouldner, A. (1954). *Patterns of Industrial Bureaucracy*. New York: Free Press.

GTC. (1996). *Gas Transmission Corporation Annual Report*.

Gunningham, N. & Johnstone, R. (1999). *Regulating Workplace Safety*. Oxford: Oxford U.P.

Gunningham, N., Johnstone, R. & Burritt, P. (1999). *Control of Major Hazard Facilities: A Report for the National Occupational Health and Safety Commission.*

Hawes, R. (1999). The buck stops where? *The Weekend Australian,* 17-18 April, 26.

Hopkins, A. (1995). *Making Safety Work: Getting Management Commitment to Occupational Health and Safety.* Sydney: Allen and Unwin.

Hopkins, A. (1999). *Managing Major Hazards: The Lessons of the Moura Mine Disaster.* Sydney: Allen & Unwin.

Hopkins, A. (1999). The privatisation of utilities: a citizen's perspective. *Australian Quarterly,* 71 (2), 30-34.

Hynes, T. & Prasad, P. (1997). Patterns of "mock bureaucracy" in mining disasters: an analysis of the Westray coal mine explosion. *Journal of Management Studies,* 34 (July), 601-623.

Johnstone, G. (1991). Report of the State Coroner of Victoria into the Fire on the Esso Offshore Oil Platform, "Tuna".

Kletz, T. (1994). *Learning from Accidents.* Oxford: Butterworth-Heinemann.

Lamm, F. (1999). OHS in NSW and Queensland small business: an overview of a NOHSC project. Paper to the ANZAOHSE Conference, 3-5 February 1999, Auckland.

LaPorte, T. & Consolini, P. (1991). Working in practice but not in theory: theoretical challenges of "high-reliability organisations". *Journal of Public Administration Research and Theory,* 1(1), 19-47.

Maidment, D. (1998). Privatisation and division into competing units as a challenge for safety management. In A. Hale & M. Baram (Ed.), *Safety Management: The Challenge of Change* (pp. 221-232). Oxford: Pergamon.

Mason, J. (1991). March v. Stramare. *Commonwealth Law Reports,* 171, 506.

Maurino, D. et al. (1995). *Beyond Aviation Human Factors.* Aldershot: Ashgate.

McNamara, P. (1999). Minister's statement. *PESA News*, (April, Victorian Supplement), 1.

Neutze, M. (1996). Competition policy, privatisation and the rights and welfare of citizens, *Citizens in the Marketplace*. Canberra: The Australia Institute, (pp. 11-21).

Neutze, M. (1997). *Funding Urban Services*. Sydney: Allen & Unwin.

NOHSC. (1996a). *Control of Major Hazard Facilities: National Standard*. Canberra: AGPS.

NOHSC. (1996b). *Economic Impact Analysis of the National Standard for Major Hazard Facilities*. Canberra: AGPS.

Perrow, C. (1982). The President's Commission and the Normal Accident. In D. Sils, C. Wolf & V. Shelanski (Ed.), *Accident at Three Mile Island: The Human Dimensions*. Boulder: Westview.

Perrow, C. (1984). *Normal Accidents: Living With High-Risk Technologies*. New York: Basic.

Perrow, C. (1999). *Normal Accidents (With New Afterword)*. Princeton: Princeton U.P.

Pidgeon, N. (1997). The limits to safety? Culture, politics, learning and man-made disasters. *Journal of Contingencies and Crisis Management, 5*(1), 1-14.

Porter, S. & Wettig, J. (1999). Policy issues on the control of major accident hazards and the new Seveso II directive. *Journal of Hazardous Materials, 65*, 1-14.

Prescott, J. (1994). A matter of safety. *BHP Review, 72*(1)

Quiggin, J. et al. (1998). *The Privatisation of ACTEW*. Canberra: The Australia Institute.

Rasmussen, J. (1997). Risk management in a dynamic society: A modelling problem. *Safety Science, 27*(2/3), 183-213.

Rasmussen, J. (1990). Human error and the problem of causality in analysis of accidents. *Phil. Trans. Royal. Soc. London,* B 327, 449-462.

Reason, J. (1997). *Managing the Risks of Organisational Accidents*. Aldershot: Ashgate.

Rees, J. (1994). *Hostages of Each Other: The Transformation of Nuclear Safety Since Three Mile Island*. Chicago: Univ of Chicago Press.

Seymour, C. (1997). Safety improvement at BHP – impact of the Moura No. 2 accident. *Journal of the Institute of Mining*, (October), 255-57.

Smith, M. (1997). Esso Australia's approach to safety management. *Proceedings of the Queensland Mining Industry Health and Safety Conference*.

Stone, C. (1975). *Where the Law Ends: The Social Control of Corporate Behaviour*. New York: Harper & Row

Toombs, S. & Whytle, D. (1998). Capital fights back: risk, regulation and profit in the UK offshore oil industry. *Studies in Political Economy*, 57 (Autumn), 73-101.

Towler, M. (1997). The perils of the performance culture. *Complete Safety Australia*, (2), 12.

Turner, B. (1978). *Man-Made Disasters*. London: Wykeham.

Vaughan, D. (1996). *The Challenger Launch Decision: Risky Technology, Culture and Deviance at NASA*. London: Univ of Chicago Press.

VWA (Victorian WorkCover Authority). (1996). *OHS Management System Audit of Esso Australia*.

VWA (Victorian WorkCover Authority). (1999a). *Proposed Occupational Health and Safety (Major Hazard Facilities) Regulations: Draft Regulations*. Melbourne: VWA.

VWA (Victorian WorkCover Authority). (1999b). *Proposed Occupational Health and Safety (Major Hazard Facilities) Regulations: Regulatory Impact Statement*. Melbourne: VWA.

Weick, K., Sutcliffe, K. & Obstfeld. (1999). Organising for high reliability: processes of collective mindfulness. *Research in Organisational Behaviour*, 21, 81-123.

Whyte, D. (1997). Moving the goalposts: The deregulation of safety in the post-Piper Alpha offshore oil industry. In J. Stanyer & G.

Stoker (Ed.), *Contemporary Political Studies* (pp. 1148-1160). Nottingham: Political Studies Association of the UK.

Wynne, B. (1988). Unruly technology: practical rules, impractical discourses and public understanding. *Social Studies of Science*, 18, 147-167.

Index

B

C

E

F

G